Corrie ten Boom

Corrie ten Boom

Jean Watson

hardback ISBN 978-1-5271-1159-2
ebook ISBN 978-1-5271-1235-3

10 9 8 7 6 5 4 3 2 1

Previously published as
Corrie ten Boom: The Watchmaker's Daughter
978-1-85792-116-8
in the Trail Blazers series.

This edition
published in 2024 by
Christian Focus Publications Ltd,
Geanies House, Fearn, Ross-shire, IV20 1TW, Great Britain.

www.christianfocus.com

Cover design by Laura K. Sayers
Printed by Gutenberg, Malta

Author's Note:
This is a true story. The people in it are real and the things that happen to them in this book actually took place. The more important conversations are based on what the people really did say at the time, as far as I have been able to discover this. The less important conversations, like the chats at mealtimes, and some background details, I have had to imagine where these are not known to me.

Contents

⏰ SMALL SCHOOLGIRL ⏰

The little girl raced along the pavement. One hand trying to hold together her unbuttoned grey coat, the other keeping the wide-brimmed hat on top of her head. All around her rose the tall, narrow houses of Old Haarlem town. They were crowded closely together, their steep roofs and crooked chimneys dark against a pearly sky.

School was over for another day. She was getting used to it, but it could never be as good as home. Her black-booted feet pounded along. Not far to go now. She clattered over the cobbles of the big market-square, with its beautiful old buildings, and then ran up another street.

There it was at last – the tall, thin corner-house, opposite the fur-shop. Past the bakers, the dress-shop and the optician's she sped, and there she was – puffing and panting outside her father's ground-floor shop, with its little white card which said 'ten Boom watches'. She peered through the window.

'Good – no customers.' she thought, and pushed open the door. The bell tinkled and her father looked up and smiled. He was standing by a glass-topped counter which was full of watches.

'Ah, Corrie.' he said, coming forward to welcome his daughter. Corrie always felt happy in this room full of busily-ticking clocks and watches. She walked over to her father and snuggled up against him. She felt so safe with his strong arms round her, and liked the smell of his jacket and the way his beard tickled her cheek when he kissed her. After a moment, he let her go and asked, 'Did you have a good day?'

'Yes, thank you, papa. I'm on a new reading book. Did you have lots of customers?'

'Not very many, Corrie, so I had time to work on this,' he said, picking up the watch he had been holding when she'd first come in, and looking at it with a pleased smile. Corrie had a look at it, too.

'It's beautiful, papa.' she exclaimed.

'It certainly is,' he agreed. 'And Mr Smit, the owner, will be very happy to have it back. He was told by a watchmaker in Amsterdam that it couldn't be mended, but it's working again now.'

Corrie wasn't at all surprised. Her papa was the best watchmaker in all of Holland, she was certain.

She often watched him at work. Sometimes he would stop for a moment and say quietly, 'Lord, I have a problem with this watch. You understand watches better than I do. I ask you to help me now.' Then his big, gentle hands would pick up the tiny parts and lovingly, patiently put them together again.

The shop bell tinkled and a man came in.

'See you later, papa,' Corrie called, as she walked to the back of the shop, while her father greeted his customer.

She went through the workroom quietly, so as not to disturb the apprentice busy at his bench, and into the hall. A girl, a little older than herself, was standing there, unbuttoning her coat.

'Oh, hullo, Nollie.' said Corrie, then she called out, 'Mama, I'm back. Where are you?'

'In the bedroom,' a voice answered from above. 'Better hang your coat up first,' said Nollie, in a motherly tone. 'And where's your hat? Don't tell me you've left it behind again?'

'It probably came off when I was hugging papa. I'll get it later,' Corrie answered, casually. She wriggled out of her coat, flung it over a peg and made for the stairs. Behind her, Nollie tutted fondly and hung the garment up properly.

Corrie pounded up the narrow, twisting stairs, humming happily.

'Really, Corrie.' A severe voice just above put a stop to her progress and her song.

'Sorry, Aunt Bep,' the girl said, standing aside. Her aunt's mouth was set in a thin, hard line. Her eyes looked bad-tempered. She walked past remarking, 'When will you learn not to rush about the house? The Waller children never did.'

Corrie climbed the rest of the way to the first floor a little more slowly, then made for the small back bedroom.

At a desk below the window sat a woman with dark, wavy hair, a fine-boned face and large, sparkling blue eyes. She turned her chair round as Corrie came in and the little girl ran into her arms and settled comfortably on her lap.

'And how's my youngest daughter?'

'All right, thank you, mama. I did ten skips without stopping and the teacher said my writing was very neat.'

'Good girl. Now, shall I tell you where I've been today? To visit Mrs van Dyer's new baby daughter. She's so sweet. I took her the shawl you used to wear when you were little, and some bootees Aunt Bep knitted.'

At the mention of her aunt, Corrie's lively, interested expression changed to a scowl, and she exclaimed, 'I'm sick of those Waller children.'

Her mother stroked her straight, brown hair and said soothingly, 'I wouldn't let them bother you, Corrie.'

'Well, she's always talking about them.'

'I know, dear, but try to remember that my sister has had a hard life as a children's nanny, and now that she is weak and sick, she needs our love and care.'

'All right, I'll try. Are you feeling all right today?'

'Yes, thank you. Just a bit tired, so I might have a lie down in a minute. But I wanted to write a note on Mrs Beuker's card. It's her birthday tomorrow, so I'll call round with a pot of Aunt Anna's jam.'

Corrie felt suddenly very hungry.

'I think I'll see what's cooking,' she said, getting up and going towards the door.

'All right, dear,' said her mother, with a laugh.

Corrie clattered down the stairs to the ground floor.

'Hullo, Aunt Anna,' she said, breezing into the kitchen and over to the big, black stove, where her aunt, looking very flushed, was stirring something in a large cooking pot. Her sleeves were rolled up and a spotless apron was fastened round her wide waist.

She had come to help her sister, Cor, after the birth of Betsie, the oldest of the ten Boom children, and had stayed ever since.

'Hungry, as usual, I suppose,' she remarked, with a fond smile at her youngest niece.

'Starving.' answered Corrie. 'This stew smells good.'

'Keep an eye on it for me, please,' said Aunt Anna, handing her the wooden spoon. Then she bustled across to the table and started chopping up vegetables. Corrie stirred the mixture in the pot, while watching her aunt's skill with the big kitchen knife.

After a short silence she said, 'I wish I could stay home and help you, instead of going to school.'

Her aunt laughed. 'I miss you, too,' she said. 'It seems funny not having anyone to lick out my mixing bowls or asking questions. I still haven't got used to the idea that you're at school now. Seems like only yesterday that you were the tiny shivering mite I used to wrap up in my apron and carry round with me while I worked.'

Corrie grinned. She never grew tired of hearing how her aunt had made a cosy nest for her as a newborn baby.

'Glad you're making yourself useful, little sister,' said a gently teasing voice from the doorway.

Betsie. Corrie turned to beam at her pretty teenage sister with her chestnut waves and brown eyes.

'Hullo, Betsie,' said Aunt Anna. 'Is Willem back, too?'

'I think so, Aunt Anna. Would you like me to lay the table for you?'

'Yes, please. No visitors for a change, so that'll be nine, unless Jans decides to eat in her room.'

'Is she sick?' asked Betsie.

'No,' answered her aunt. 'It's just that she might be rather tired when she gets back from shopping.'

'Shopping.' echoed Betsie in dismay. 'I hope she's not buying hats or dresses for us.'

11

Corrie didn't mind what she wore as long as it was comfortable and didn't slow her down too much, but her sisters had their own ideas about clothes – and these were not the same as their aunt's.

'If Jans chooses to spend her money on you, be grateful,' Aunt Anna chided, gently. Betsie flushed and answered quickly, 'It's very generous of her, I know, but I wish she'd choose pretty, bright colours.'

'Perhaps she will,' said Corrie, hopefully, hating to see her sister upset. Betsie smiled at her, then went towards the door saying, 'Anyway, I'll lay for nine.'

'Thank you,' said Aunt Anna. She scooped up the vegetables, walked over to the cooking pot, and threw them in. Corrie handed the spoon back to her and watched her aunt mixing everything up while she thought about her mother's third sister, Aunt Jans, who had moved into their two big front rooms on the second floor after her husband's death.

'She means to be kind and she's clever,' she thought, 'but I wish she wasn't so bossy. And the fuss she makes when she's ill. Mama's often sick, but she doesn't fuss at all.'

'I wonder if you and Nollie would mind fetching me some cheese from the shop?' asked Aunt Anna.

'Of course not,' said Corrie, 'I'll go and find Nollie now.' She went into the hall. A boy, a little younger than Betsie, was coming out of the workroom.

'Do you know where Nollie is, Willem?' Corrie asked him.

He looked up with rather a serious expression on his face and answered, 'I think she's in the alley.' This was the space beside the house where the ten Boom children played, since they had no garden.

Corrie went to the side door and called out to Nollie, 'Aunt Anna wants us to buy some cheese for her.' Nollie was bouncing a ball.

'Forty-eight, forty-nine, fifty,' she counted. Then she stopped bouncing and said, 'All right.'

Corrie skipped along beside her sister. The pavements were fairly full of people walking about and the streets were busy with bicycles. Now and then, the tinkling of their bells mingled with the clatter of hooves and the rumble of wheels, as the horse-drawn trolley buses moved along the street.

The girls bought a portion of golden cheese and started home. It was then that they noticed the little group of children obviously mocking someone.

They squirmed to the front to see who it was.

There stood 'crazy Thys' – as everyone called him. Corrie had often seen this backward boy ambling about the streets in his ragged clothes. Now he was standing still, looking bewildered and helpless as the children round him made unkind remarks and laughed at him.

Corrie felt very sad first of all and then angry.

'Stop it. Leave him alone.' she shouted.

There was a sudden silence. The children turned to stare at the speaker and saw a small girl with flashing blue eyes. Crazy Thys was looking at her, too. Then he walked over and kissed her. She was just thinking that he had a funny smell, when Nollie grabbed her by the hand and started pulling her away from the square.

'Hurry,' she shouted, dragging her little sister along the street as fast as she could.

They arrived home, and Nollie pulled her breathless companion inside, shouting, 'Quickly, everyone. Dirty Thys has kissed our Corrie. Come and wash her clean.'

Corrie now began to feel scared.

Aunt Jans was on her way down the stairs and she hurried towards her nieces and was joined by Aunt Bep from the dining room. They took Corrie into the kitchen and scrubbed her cheeks, while asking Nollie what had happened.

The moment they let her go, the little girl ran upstairs to find her mother. She was lying down and Corrie climbed on to the bed, snuggled against her and poured out her story, adding, 'Mamma, why was it wrong for crazy Thys to kiss me? They were all making fun of him.'

'Dear Corrie,' said her mother, stroking a flushed cheek, 'Jesus has given you this love for poor Thys and others like him, and I'm glad. But sometimes people who haven't come to love Jesus, do bad things. So it's best not to get too close to them. Just pray for Thys.'

Corrie felt a bit better.

Soon it was time for the evening meal. When nine people were sitting round the oval dining room table, Corrie's father closed his eyes and said, 'Lord, we thank you for this food, and we ask that you will bless our Queen, and that the Lord Jesus will come again soon.'

Then the eating and the talking began. Corrie still felt a bit shaky inside, so she didn't say much, but she managed to tuck into her plateful of stew.

'Did you get your shopping done, Jans?' asked Corrie's mother. Betsie and Nollie exchanged glances.

'Yes, thank you, Cor,' her sister replied. 'I bought myself a thick coat as well as a hat and scarf. So I hope

I won't get so many colds this winter through having to speak in draughty church halls.'

Corrie saw her sisters looking very relieved, then Nollie remarked, 'Our teacher said a funny thing today. He said Holland's oldest enemy and best friend was water.'

'Quite right,' commented her father. 'Water makes Holland green and fertile.' Corrie nearly asked what 'fertile' meant, but then Willem said, 'And it's why there are so many good Dutch engineers and builders – so I think it's more of a friend than an enemy.'

'As long as it stays where we want it to and doesn't flood our land,' said Betsie.

'Talking of land,' put in Aunt Jans, who had been waiting rather impatiently for a chance to speak, 'have any of you seen those new houses on the edge of Haarlem?'

The conversation flowed on. Empty plates were cleared away and a delicious, fluffy lemon pudding was served and enjoyed.

'Another excellent meal, Anna,' said Corrie's father.

'Thank you, Casper,' said his sister-in-law.

Corrie watched her father taking down and opening the big, black family Bible. He handled it as though it were a very precious watch.

Tonight he opened it near the middle and read a psalm about not being afraid. He said a few words about it and prayed.

Corrie felt much better now. If God and papa said not to be afraid, that was good enough for her.

By bedtime she was her usual happy self. She shared a bedroom with Nollie on the third floor. There were four other little bedrooms up there, and Betsie, Willem, Aunt Bap and Aunt Anna had one each.

Corrie got into her nightie, then called down the banisters, 'I'm ready, papa.' By the time he had climbed up to her room, she was in bed, waiting for him to listen to her prayers.

He knelt down and she said, 'Dear Lord, bless mama and make her well and strong. And please bless papa and Betsie and Willem and Nollie and me, and the aunts and all our friends. And I also ask you to bless crazy Thys.'

Her father got up to kiss her and tuck her in.

'Goodnight, Corrie, I love you,' he said, putting a hand on her cheek.

She lay quite still, not wanting to lose the feel of his hand, while he went out of the room and down the stairs.

In a few moments, she fell happily asleep.

⏱ MISCHIEVOUS TOMBOY ⏱

Autumn in Haarlem had its own magic, when the leaves on the poplars turned to gold and the street lamps were lit earlier and cast strange shadows around. Corrie played indoors mostly then.

'Ninety-nine, a hundred. Coming – ready or not.' she shouted, opening her eyes and looking right and left along the pews for any sign of her friend Dot.

Suddenly, a head bobbed up over the little door at the end of a nearby pew. The next moment, the two girls were racing down the aisle, giggling furiously.

'Home. O-u-t spells out,' panted Corrie, touching a huge stone pillar a few seconds before Dot reached it. 'Now it's my turn to hide.'

St. Bavo's cathedral, towering over the market-square, rang with their laughing voices and running feet.

Dot's father, who was Corrie's Uncle Arnold, looked after the beautiful, old church with its curved Gothic windows and famous pipe-organ. The ten Booms went into this building every Sunday to worship God together. Now and then, as a special treat, they heard organ recitals, too. But when there were no services or concerts on, Uncle Arnold let the girls play in and out of the pews. These places were just right for hide-and-seek, or for playing at being shopkeepers, teachers, explorers ...

One night snow fell from a lead-covered sky. In the morning, Corrie looked out at a dazzling carpet spread across the flat fields, where millions of bulbs lay hidden under straw. The snow fell on ponds, canals and ditches to form glittering sheets of ice. It decorated windmill sails, rooftops and chimney stacks to make a sparkling playground of the cobbled market-square and streets.

Corrie and Dot were soon out-of-doors, crunching through untouched snow, slithering over well-trodden, hard patches, skating across icy ditches.

'This is just the right snow for making snowballs,' commented Corrie. They scooped up handfuls of the powdery flakes, patted them into balls, then pushed them into their coat pockets and walked along.

Round a corner they skimmed. Ahead of them were three gentlemen, talking busily. They were wearing smart coats and tall top hats. Corrie and Dot looked at each other, their eyes bright with mischief.

Each slid a hand into her pocket and pulled out a snowball, took aim and fired. Two white balls shot through the air, knocking off two of the top hats.

The gentlemen tutted with annoyance and looked round for the culprits. Dot and Corrie scooted towards the fallen hats, picked them up and dusted them off.

'Where could those scamps have disappeared to?' said one man.

'Here you are, sir,' said Corrie, presenting him with his hat and smiling sweetly. Dot did the same to the other hatless man.

'Thank you. What good young ladies you are.' the gentlemen said, smiling at the girls with their bright eyes and innocent faces.

Corrie and Dot walked quickly away. When they were safely out of sight, they exploded into laughter.

Winter was fun in Haarlem. But then, so was spring, when crocuses, daffodils and tulips painted wide bands of orange, blue, yellow and white across the fields, and the pavements were carpeted with fallen cherry blossom.

'Hurry, Corrie, I've something to show you.' Dot said, one morning. Corrie called out goodbye to her family and joined her friend in the alley. The girls moved away from the house and then Dot fished something out of her pocket. It was a coin, snapped in two.

'A tram must have run over it,' said Corrie.

'If I do this,' said Dot, pushing the pieces together, 'you'd hardly think it was broken, would you?'

'No, you wouldn't,' agreed Corrie.

'We could buy ten whole sweets with it,' said Dot. Corrie ignored the prickly feeling inside her. Instead, she pictured herself eating a big, juicy, delicious sweet, and then another, and another ...

'I'll ask for the sweets and you put the money down – right?' said Dot.

Corrie nodded. They hurried off to the sweet shop with beating hearts. The bell tinkled as they walked in.

'Hullo, young ladies. What can I do for you?' the shop-lady greeted them. She was pleasant with a jolly smile.

'May we have ten of those sweets?' asked Dot, pointing to some large, coloured balls.

'Certainly,' the lady answered. She took down the jar and counted out the right number. As Dot scooped them up, Corrie laid the broken coin on the counter. Then both girls scooted.

They were some distance down the streets before they heard the shop bell tinkling and the lady's voice calling, 'Girls, girls, come back.'

Ignoring her, they kept running, until they were safely inside the school playground. There they stood, panting, while Dot counted five sweets into Corrie's hand.

Each girl popped a sweet into her mouth and began sucking it noisily. Neither spoke for a moment, and then Corrie said stickily, 'Mine tastes funny.'

'So does mine,' admitted Dot.

Corrie's prickly feeling was back, and she thought, 'I'll never try anything like this again.'

But there were other kinds of fun ...

With the seaside not far away, summer brought trips to the warm, silky sand dunes, and the chance to tumble in and out of the sparkling blue water. Of course, there was always school after the holidays, but Corrie found some of the lessons quite interesting. She wasn't clever, like Willem and Nollie, but she had plenty of friends and a head brimful of ideas.

***

'Keep working quietly. I shall be back soon,' Mr van Ree said to his class of ten-year olds, as he left the room. When he had gone, the girls started talking quietly.

'I've got an idea.' Corrie announced, as loudly as she dared.

'Go on,' urged Dot. Corrie looked round at the eager faces of her class-mates and said, 'Wouldn't it be a joke if we all put on our hats at two this afternoon? Can't you imagine Mr van Ree's face?'

There were stifled giggles and a chorus of 'Yes' and 'Good idea – let's do it.'

Then someone thought of a problem.

'But we have to leave our hats in the coat cupboard,' she pointed out.

'Well, we'll just have to smuggle them into the classroom somehow,' said Dot, 'and hide them in our desks till it's time to put them on.'

'How will we know when it's two o'clock?' another asked. Corrie proudly showed them her watch.

'I'll give a signal,' she said, 'I know – I'll scratch my head like this, and you'll know that it's time then.

At almost two o'clock, Mr van Ree looked suspiciously round, thinking, 'They're not usually quite so industrious. I wonder what's up.' But he couldn't see anything amiss, and didn't notice that the girl in the front row kept glancing at her wrist watch.

Two o'clock at last. Corrie gave the signal, took out from her desk the sailor hat which Aunt Jans had bought for her, and put it on her head.

There was no sound or movement behind her. She darted a quick look round – and froze in horror. Every girl was hatless, except for herself, right at the front, and one other girl, right at the back.

'Now I'm for it.' she thought, forcing herself to look up. Mr van Ree was glaring straight at her.

'Corrie ten Boom,' he thundered, 'go and see Mr van Lyden at once.' Corrie gave a gasp of horror and her cheeks turned white. Somehow, she managed to get up from her seat and leave the classroom.

Outside in the corridor, she wondered which was worse – disobeying Mr van Ree, or going to see the headmaster? She knew that Mr van Lyden was very strict. He sometimes expelled people. She couldn't risk that so she crept off to hide in the coat cupboard. The soft fabrics caught her tears and muffled her sobs.

'Why did the others let me down? Will that bell never go?' she wondered miserably. What was she to do?

The bell rang at last. Corrie snatched up her things and was outside in a flash. Through the school gate and down the road she flew. If only she could have run into papa or mama's arms – everything would have been all right. But they mustn't know.

As soon as she was home, she ran up to her room and threw herself on the bed which she and Nollie shared.

'Who will help me?' she wondered. 'Betsie's so good and gentle. I couldn't bear to hurt her. Willem would make me own up. That leaves Nollie. She'll help me. But I'll have to wait till bedtime to get her on her own.'

'Is that you, Corrie?' called a voice from below.

'Yes, mama. I'm just coming,' her daughter replied, trying to sound normal. She went down the stairs thinking, 'I'll have to pretend everything's all right.'

The rest of the day seemed to drag by.

Corrie was only half-listening to what people were saying that night. Betsie's class had spent the afternoon at the Frans Hals Museum and she was full of the visit.

'There were so many beautiful things there.' she exclaimed, her eyes shining, 'and the paintings were marvellous – especially the ones showing the Dutch countryside. You must come and see for yourselves.'

'A family treat. What a lovely idea.' said her mother, who shared Betsie's love of beautiful things.

'Holland has many fine painters,' said her father, with quiet pride.

'And musicians,' said Willem.

'And bored soldiers – judging by the streets of Haarlem,' cut in Aunt Jans, dramatically. Everyone turned to look at her and she continued, 'Haven't you noticed the men in uniform loafing about our streets?'

'There are quite a number about,' agreed Corrie's father. 'I must have cycled past a dozen or so on my rounds this afternoon.'

'Satan finds some mischief still for idle hands to do,' commented Aunt Bep, gloomily.

Corrie noticed the twinkle in her father's eye. He and mama seemed to be sharing a secret joke.

'Exactly, Bep.' exclaimed her sister. 'And that's why I have decided to start a club for our Dutch soldiers. I shall organise meetings, sports, camps, competitions ...'

'Aren't you feeling well, Corrie?' her mother asked, kindly.

'I'm all right, mama,' the girl said lifting a glass of milk to her lips. It hid her face while she drank.

After the meal, Casper took down the family Bible and led prayers in his usual slow, thoughtful way. Then he said, 'A few of our friends are coming round to join us for a musical evening, so we shall have a happy time together, singing and making music. I hope I shall have the pleasure of hearing my children sing something.'

Corrie's heart sank even lower. Music, singing and visitors. On any other evening, she would have enjoyed them all as much as the others, but not tonight.

She sat in the middle of her family and their friends, feeling sad and lonely, while her father puffed contentedly on his cigar, and the music of Bach filled the room.

At last it was her bedtime. Her father listened to her prayers and tucked her into bed.

'Goodnight, Corrie, I love you,' he said, laying a hand on her cheek.

She felt like crying, but she managed to blink back the tears and say goodnight to him.

When he had gone, she prayed, 'Dear Lord, please forgive me for being so naughty, and please, please don't let me hurt mama or papa. Amen.' The tears trickled down her cheeks as she lay in bed, waiting for Nollie.

The moment her sister's neat, little figure appeared round the door, Corrie sat up and started pouring out her story. Nollie came and sat on the bed to listen, her pretty face very serious. She was a good, clever child, hardly ever in trouble herself, but she felt sorry for her sad, mischievous little sister and wanted to help her.

Corrie finished her story and asked, 'Oh, Nollie, what shall I do?'

'You must ask God to forgive you,' said Nollie, in a serious grown-up voice.

'Oh, I've already done that,' answered Corrie. Her sister had another idea.

'You know that psalm papa was reading tonight about people crying to God in their trouble – well, shall we try doing that?' she said.

Corrie nodded. Then shut her eyes and prayed earnestly, 'O Lord, I am in trouble and so I am crying to you for help.'

'Just like you helped the people in that psalm,' added Nollie. Both girls said, 'Amen', and went to bed.

***

'Corrie, wake up.'

Corrie opened her eyes about half-way and saw Nollie bending over her, saying, 'I've had a good idea.'

'What's she talking about?' thought Corrie, groggily. Then everything came back to her in a rush, and she opened her eyes wide and saw that it was morning.

'Go on,' she urged.

'Well, you know those missionary magazines we help to deliver,' Nollie began.

'Yes,'

'And you know Mr van Lyden always has one.'

'Yes.'

'Why don't you take him his magazine? You never know, it might do some good,' Nollie finished. Corrie thought about the idea and decided it was worth a try.

'All right,' she said, and threw off the bedclothes.

After breakfast, they found a pile of the missionary magazines. Corrie took one and put it into her satchel. But it wasn't easy to go to the headmaster's office. Her heart was thumping madly as she knocked on his door.

'Come in,' he said, and she went in, holding the magazine in front of her like a shield, and blurted out, 'Excuse me, Mr van Lyden, but I've brought you this.'

The headmaster took the booklet, and looked straight at her for a long moment. At last he said, 'It is good of you to bring it, but I hear you weren't such a good Christian girl yesterday, Corrie ten Boom.'

The dreaded moment had come. Corrie hardly dared to breathe.

'That is all. You may go,' said Mr van Lyden.

Corrie's breath escaped in a sigh of relief.

'Thank you, sir.' she said, and left the room, feeling as though she were treading on air.

Out into the playground she floated to look for her sister.

'Nollie, Nollie, it worked.' she exclaimed, when she saw her. 'I cried to God in my trouble, and he helped me. He really did. Oh, thank you, Nollie. I'm so happy I could fly.'

⏱ YOUNG WOMAN ⏱

'Please let me look good, just for today.' wished Corrie, as Betsie finished doing her hair.

'There.' said her elder sister at last. 'Take a look.' Corrie moved gingerly across to the full-length mirror. What she saw in it made her mouth open in surprise.

'Heavens. Is this really me?' she thought, faced with the reflection of an attractive young woman with sparkling blue eyes, matching silk dress, and curly swept-up hair.

Betsie came to stand behind her, and said, 'You look lovely.' Corrie blushed with pleasure, then turned to squeeze her sister's hands, and said, 'Thanks for making my dress, and doing my hair, and everything, Betsie.'

'That's all right,' said her sister, smiling. 'I'll just go and see if Nollie's all right. Promise me that you'll keep still until it's time to go.'

'I promise,' answered Corrie, blithely. She stared at herself and thought, 'I'll never be really beautiful, like Betsie and Nollie, but today I do look all right, and I'm so glad about that, because today I shall see Karel again.' Her thoughts flew back seven years to one of her mother's parties.

'Corrie, I'd like you to meet a friend of mine from university – Karel. Karel, meet my youngest sister,' Willem had said. Blue eyes had stared up into brown ones – and Corrie had promptly fallen in love. It had happened before, but never quite like that.

They hadn't seen much of each other over the years, for he was busy studying theology at Leiden university with Willem, and she was busy at home. But his name and face had stayed in her mind, like a secret spring of joy, while she helped with the cooking and housework, studied, taught Bible classes, went to missionary conferences for young people – and grew from child into woman.

There had been some changes in her life at home. Aunt Bep had died of tuberculosis, her mother suffered more and more often with her stomach trouble, and Aunt Jans had got diabetes. But this was a day for joy. Willem and Tine were to be married, and Karel would be at the wedding.

'Time to go,' said Betsie, coming back into the room.

She saw him standing outside the church, and then he saw her.

'Corrie?' he said, a little uncertainly, for the young woman coming towards him was quite unlike Willem's kid-sister, as he remembered her.

'That's right,' Corrie answered gaily.

'Grown into a lovely lady,' commented Karel.

He gave her his arm, and she floated into the church on a cloud of happiness.

There was no sleep for her that night. She lay wide awake dreaming of another wedding day – a day when she would be the white-gowned bride, and Karel her handsome groom.

She was twenty-one now, and Karel twenty-six. He'd finished his studies, so there was nothing to stop him getting married, if he wanted to.

'Oh, Karel, Karel, when will I see you again?' her heart sang out ...

June came, and every window box on the bridges and houses of Haarlem blazed with colour. Corrie and her family packed their things, and went off to stay for a few days in the village of Made, where Willem had been appointed as preacher and minister.

The year had begun rather sadly with Aunt Jans' death in February, but it had been wonderful to see her lose all fear and die peacefully, trustingly, in the end.

And now they had come to hear Willem preach his first sermon. His house was opposite the church. Corrie roamed around the rooms, waiting impatiently for the doorbell to ring.

There it was at last. She flew down to open it. Seeing the tall, dark, handsome figure made her feel suddenly very fluttery.

'Oh, Karel, come in. I'll go and get Willem,' she said, all in a rush.

'Corrie, it's a beautiful day. Come for a walk,' said Karel, dropping his case in the hall.

'Oh, yes,' she answered, eagerly.

They strolled along country lanes, talking.

The meadows around them glowed with summer flowers, and above their heads the clouds were gilt-edged.

Willem's mood did not match Corrie's. He talked a lot about the war in Europe.

'Holland may be neutral,' he said in his first sermon, 'but our country will be affected by what is happening in the rest of Europe. Our whole way of life is changing.'

'Oh, Willem,' thought Corrie, 'why must you always be so gloomy? I want to be happy.'

She was sitting in Willem and Tine's front room, dreaming, one afternoon. Karel was in the village, but would soon be back.

She could see it all – Karel, and herself in a cosy little house with their children. (She wanted six, but Karel thought four would be enough.) He would be a fine preacher and she would be such a good wife, helping him with his work and bringing up their family ...

Willem's voice broke in on her dreams. 'Er, Corrie.'

He and Tine had just come into the room and were standing near her. Corrie tore her thoughts away from the rosy future, and focused on her brother and sister-in-law.

'Yes,' she said.

Willem sat down and his wife perched beside him.

'Er, there's something I think I ought ...' her brother began, but Corrie interrupted him.

'What is it, Willem?' she asked, puzzled.

It wasn't at all like him to beat about the bush, so she wondered what was coming. Both he and Tine looked rather uncomfortable, she thought.

'I hope,' said Willem, still sounding strangely hesitant, 'Karel hasn't given you the impression that you and he could – um – get serious about each other?'

Corrie flushed bright scarlet, and opened her mouth to speak, but no words came.

'The fact is,' continued Willem, 'Karel's parents – and particularly his mother – have made up their minds that their son will marry someone rich and fashionable.'

Corrie mumbled something and got away from Willem as quickly as she could. Into the garden she went, and as she walked along the paths between the flower beds, her heart was saying, 'Oh Willem, you're wrong, you're wrong. I will marry Karel and be happy – you'll see.'

A few more happy, sunlit walks and it was time for the visitors to leave. 'Write to me, Corrie,' said Karel. She smiled up at him and promised that she would, while thinking, 'Though you didn't need to ask, Karel, my love.'

***

Back in Haarlem there was so much to do, but Corrie found time to write pages and pages of letters to Karel. His letters answered hers at first, and then tailed off.

'It's his job,' she told herself. 'He has a big church and parish to look after, so he can't have much free time.'

The summer faded and was followed by the splendours of autumn, and the sharp, bright days of early winter, when a clear, silvery light put a sheen on each leafless tree, each cobbled street and waterway ...

The doorbell rang and Corrie went to open it.

Karel – at last. But who was this smiling, elegant young lady leaning on his arm?

'Corrie, meet my fiancée,' said Karel.

Corrie was shattered, her dream of happiness smashed. Numbly, she said, 'Come in' and led the couple upstairs to the family parlour – once Aunt Jans' front room.

She heard herself saying, 'Karel has brought his fiancée to see us,' and saw the quick sympathy and understanding in the eyes of her family.

'Karel, my friend, there is something I want to ask you about,' said her father, and the young man went across and was soon absorbed in conversation.

'What a very beautiful hat.' Betsie commented to Karel's fiancée, and the girl was soon discussing fashions with her. Corrie was able to stay in the background, helping her mother and Aunt Anna serve coffee and cakes, while inwardly fighting to control her feelings.

At last, the visitors left. Corrie could be alone. She ran up to her bedroom and shut the door. Then she cried as she had never cried in her life. Much later, she heard her father's footsteps coming up the stairs.

'Please, please, don't let him say that I'll find someone else, when I know there'll never be anyone else for me,' Corrie prayed.

Her father came in and sat on her bed.

'Corrie,' he said, gently, 'Love is the strongest force in the world. When someone hurts our love, we can stop loving and so stop the hurting, or we can ask God to use our love in a different way. You cannot give Karel the kind of love you feel for him now, but if you ask, God will give you a new kind of love for him – his kind of love.'

He touched her shoulder lovingly, then got up and left her alone, with the memory of his presence and his words. Her world was very dark, but she now knew what she must do.

'Lord, I give you my love for Karel,' she prayed. 'Please give me your new love for him.' Then she fell into an exhausted sleep.

There was no time to mope in the busy days ahead, even if she had wanted to. Her mother had her worst stroke. She had had several minor ones and had recovered from them quite well, but this time she was left speechless and partly paralysed.

Corrie took on most of the nursing, for Betsie had anaemia and was not at all strong. Aunt Anna was beginning to feel her age. Nollie was out teaching all day and Father had the business to run.

Corrie's mother could still say one word – 'Corrie'.

But her family found ways of 'talking' with her ...

'Corrie.'

'Yes, Mama. Do you need something?'

A shake of the head, meaning 'no'.

'Is there something you want me to do?'

A nod, meaning 'yes'.

'Is it for someone in this house?'

A shake of the head.

'Someone in the street?'

A nod.

'Someone in the street has a birthday – is that it?'

More nodding.

'And you want to send a card, of course, so let me think. Is it Mrs de Hough? Mrs Beuker …?'

Sometimes Corrie would look at her mother in awe.

'Crippled, speechless and in pain, but she still lives for others,' she would think. And she could see from the expressions on the faces of their many visitors, that they too, were moved and inspired by her mother's beauty of spirit.

***

The war in Europe came to a bitter end in 1918 after four years. The ten Booms had been following its terrible progress with deep sympathy and sadness and now they talked over the new situation.

'The war may be over, but the scars will take a long time to heal,' said Corrie. Betsie nodded and added sadly, 'There must be thousands of widows and orphans all over Europe.'

'More in Germany than anywhere else,' answered her father. He stroked his greying beard and went on, 'We must do something for German orphans. I shall find loving Dutch homes for some of these poor children.'

In the next days, he contacted his watchmaking friends all over Holland and arranged everything.

The pale, thin, frightened children started arriving and were quickly welcomed into loving homes. Some came to live in the house over the watch shop. Once again, every room was full. Corrie was busier than ever.

There was another wedding in the ten Boom family. Nollie married a fellow teacher, Flip van Woerden, whom she'd met through going to teach in a school in Amsterdam. After their marriage, they went to live in one of the newer houses on the edge of Haarlem.

'Now I can think of Karel and feel no pain,' Corrie realised. God had given her a new kind of love for him and for others – her family, the boys and girls in her Bible classes, and the war orphans from Germany.

She was twenty-seven. There would never be another Karel – she knew that. And Betsie would never marry, either, because of her poor health. But life at home was still good.

***

The children went back to Germany, well, strong and happy again, but Corrie's mother grew weaker and weaker.

She died peacefully. Her husband looked down at her and said, 'This is the saddest day of my life'.

Corrie put her arms around him, thinking, 'Dear Father, I will take care of you always.'

Corrie went about her work in a haze of happy memories, tinged with sadness. Mama holding her small hand and helping her to ask Jesus into her life ... visiting the sick, the sad and the old ... putting a coin into a box whenever they had a visitor and saying, gaily, 'Welcome to our home, and because we are so glad to have you, we are adding a contribution to our missionary fund.' They were also throwing parties and planning treats.

Every room in the house, every object, stirred memories. There was the desk where she had written so many loving cards and letters, and the bed where her children had found comfort, and where she had lain so often in pain but uncomplaining. There were the clothes she had made and the pots of fuchsias and geraniums so lovingly grown on the bit of flat roof which she called her garden.

And of course, there was Father – Casper, without his precious Cor. Corrie's heart ached for him. But though his wife's death aged and saddened him, he went on being the man she had helped to make him: head of the family, respected watchmaker, loving father and grandfather, and friend to everyone in Haarlem, whether servant or rich customer.

Betsie, so like her mother in ways, was grieving too.

'Dear sister, I shall take care of you and father,' Corrie thought, fondly. 'And Aunt Anna and the three of us will be very happy together.'

⏱ WATCHMAKER ⏱

'The trouble with you, Corrie,' said Aunt Anna, 'is that you want to do six things at once.'

Corrie laughed, but she knew this was true. Aunt Anna still managed some of the cooking, but Corrie helped her, and did the housework and shopping, too, while Betsie and father took care of the shop.

Corrie loved her work, and crammed in Bible classes, meetings, missionary conferences, study and visiting.

A flu epidemic hit Haarlem one winter. Corrie caught sight of Betsie's shivering body and flushed face, and bundled her back to bed. Then she went to talk to Aunt Anna.

'Leave Betsie and the cooking to me,' this lady said, firmly.

'If you're sure you can manage,' answered Corrie. She went through to her father in the shop.

'Meet your new assistant,' she said. Behind round spectacles, his eyes twinkled. There were a few lines on his face now, but his hands were as steady as ever.

'What a blessing to have two helpful daughters,' he said. 'I'm so glad you persuaded Betsie to go to bed.'

The days flew by.

'You're looking much better,' Corrie told Betsie one evening.

'I am.' was the reply. Corrie sat down on her sister's bed for a chat.

'I still feel rather shy with the customers and I'll never be as good as you at remembering people's names and asking after their children, but it's bliss working with father – I really love it.' she said.

'I've been enjoying myself, too, doing a bit in the house,' said Betsie. 'Only pottering,' she added hastily, seeing her sister's accusing look.

'And I thought you'd been in bed.' exclaimed Corrie.

'I have been – most of the time,' said her sister.

Corrie smiled at her and said, 'Anyway, I'm just happy that you're better.' She picked up Betsie's supper tray and went down the stairs. Then she took a look round the house.

A freshly painted cupboard, a vase of flowers in the corner, a pretty cloth on a sideboard, crockery arranged artistically, ornaments on a mantelpiece – they all pointed to Betsie.

'Pottering indeed.' thought Corrie fondly. A thoughtful look came into her eyes. After a moment, she went back up the stairs to Betsie's room.

'How would you like to swop jobs for a time?' she asked.

Her sister's face told her the answer, even before she said, 'Oh, Corrie, I'd love it.'

Betsie made the house look beautiful as well as clean, while Corrie served the customers and tried to sort out the accounts. The business was not making much profit, and it didn't take her long to find one reason for this ...

'Father, has Mr Smit paid the bill for his watch? You spent hours mending it.'

'It was a pleasure to handle such a watch.'

'I know, Father. But the money – where is it?'

'Well, Corrie, that man is having a hard time at the moment. We read the Bible and prayed together.'

'Yes, Father, but the money.'

'I was just coming to that. I told Mr Smit that the work on his watch was a little gift from the Lord.'

'Oh, Father.' Corrie shook her head fondly, and gave up.

'Lord,' she prayed. 'You know what we need. Please send us the money you want us to have.'

There was food on the table at every mealtime.

***

Corrie grew more confident with the customers and mastered the paperwork. But it wasn't enough.

'Father, would you be willing to teach me to mend watches?' she asked him one day.

'But of course.' he replied, delighted. 'It would be a pleasure to teach my daughter about the things I love.'

Hours, days and months of hard work followed, but at last Corrie had some good news for her kind, patient teacher. When he heard it, his face broke into a beaming smile.

'Congratulations, Corrie. You have made me very happy.' he said. Then he shook his grey head exclaiming, 'My own daughter. The first licensed woman watchmaker in Holland. Wonderful. Wonderful.'

Corrie settled eagerly into her work as a proper watchmaker, and the days flew by.

***

Corrie had just come back from a meeting for Bible class leaders, and she was telling Betsie all about it.

'You see,' she explained, 'there are Bible classes and activities for children up to thirteen years old, and groups for over-eighteens, but nothing at all for those in between. Something must be done.'

'You sound like Aunt Jans,' said Betsie, with a smile. 'But seriously, Corrie, haven't you got enough to do?'

'Oh, I'd have lots of helpers,' Corrie told her.

The sisters talked and prayed over the idea with their father and reached a decision ...

'How did it go?' asked Betsie, eagerly. Corrie had just come back from an evening with 'her girls'. Her sister and father supported and prayed for the new venture.

'Very well, thank you,' Corrie answered. 'We had gymnastics this evening, and then I gave a short Bible talk, and everyone seemed to be listening well.'

'Good.' commented her father, smiling. 'What a success this Haarlem Girls' Club is proving to be.'

'Yes, but isn't it a shame there's nothing for boys of this age group?' said Corrie. 'I'd like to invite them to join us.'

'Mixed clubs.' exclaimed Betsie. 'What a good idea. But I'm afraid some people won't approve.'

The clubs grew. Corrie spent all her spare time organising hobbies, sports, camps, and training leaders. Betsie was busy, too. Aunt Anna became too weak and ill to work in the kitchen and had to stay in bed, so she had the cooking to do. As the sisters went about their work, they could hear the great old lady singing all the hymns she knew and loved.

One day the singing stopped, and the singer went to be with her Lord.

'I'll miss dear Aunt Anna,' said Betsie. 'But I'm glad she's with Mother.'

The whole family and many friends gathered for the funeral.

***

Willem was a frequent visitor. He had left the preaching ministry and was now in charge of a nursing home for old people in Hilversum.

'Corrie,' he said one day, 'as you know, I'm on the board of a missionary society. Well, right now we need homes for three children. Their parents are missionaries about to go abroad.'

Corrie and Betsie talked it over. They had always been interested in missionary work – and in children.

'Besides,' said Betsie, 'Father would be so happy to hear children's voices in our home again.'

And so the children came – three to begin with, and then more and more until there were seven being cared for by 'Opa', 'Aunt Kees' and 'Aunt Betsie', as they called Casper and his daughters.

Over the next ten years, the house rang with their young voices.

'Opa, can you show me how this watch works?'

'Aunt Kees, let's go for a picnic.'

'Aunt Betsie, what's for supper?'

Corrie organised their sports and hobbies, and was happy for them to join in with any of her club activities.

Betsie took care of their food and clothes, and they all adored 'Opa' who still led family prayers every day.

'Corrie, you do so many things,' her father told her one day. 'But when we get to heaven, it wouldn't surprise me to discover that the work you do for handicapped people is the most important of all.'

This was just the encouragement Corrie needed. Forgetting her tiredness, she set off to visit a boy called Henk who was a member of her class for backward children. He had ten brothers and sisters and came from a poor family. His job was making clothes pegs in a government workshop. Like all the others in the class he listened eagerly when Corrie said, 'Jesus loves you. He cares for each of you. You are precious to him.'

She reached the little house and knocked on the door with the faded paint. Henk's mother opened it. She looked very worn.

'Oh, hullo – it's Miss ten Boom, isn't it? Come in. I expect you've come to see Henk,' she said.

'That's right,' said Corrie, stepping inside. She had to raise her voice above the din made by some of Henk's brothers and sisters as she asked, 'How is he?'

'Same as usual,' the woman replied. 'No trouble at all, our Henk. Stays in his room, good as gold, he does. You can go up if you like.'

'Thank you,' said Corrie. She climbed the stairs towards Henk's tiny attic room, but before she reached it, she could hear the singing.

'Out of my bondage, sorrow and night, Jesus I come, Jesus I come,' sang the sweet, young voice. Corrie tiptoed to the door of his room and looked inside.

Henk had his back to her. He was on his knees in front of a chair. Propped up against the back of it was a tattered picture. It showed Jesus on the cross. Henk was looking at the picture and singing the hymn as though nothing else in the world mattered.

Corrie tiptoed back down the stairs, tears in her eyes. The cramped room had been a little bit of heaven, because God's love had been there. She had almost seen the angels.

'I didn't want to disturb him,' she explained to Henk's mother, and then went home.

***

Corrie's little group of handicapped children were arriving for their class. Henk was not among them, and Corrie knew why. Someone had just given her a message from Henk's mother to say that the little boy was dead. She had found him kneeling by a chair, holding on to a picture of Jesus.

Corrie was feeling sad and happy at the same time, but the happiness was stronger, for she could picture Henk slipping into the presence of Jesus in the middle of singing 'Out of my bondage, sorrow and night, Jesus, I come to thee.'

The children had all settled down and were looking at her now. She gave them a warm smile, and said, 'I am so glad to see you, and today I have a very special story for you …'

***

The years passed – busy, peaceful years. Only Corrie, her father and older sister were at home now, but Nollie and

Flip and their growing family lived near enough to pop in. Willem and Tine and their children came over from Hilversum as often as they could.

Corrie was forty-five years old when she and Betsie had a party to celebrate the hundredth birthday of the watch shop. Family, friends and neighbours poured in with flowers, cards and presents for the old man they all loved so much. It was a day to remember.

Father ten Boom went to bed, tired but happy. 'The Lord has given me many blessings,' he said. 'My work, home, children, grandchildren, and all our friends.' He paused, before adding the words he often said: 'And the best is yet to be.'

The last visitor had left and the dishes had been washed up and put away.

'Well, Betsie,' said Corrie, as the sisters sat sipping a hot bedtime drink, 'our future seems clear enough. We shall stay at home, looking after Father, and growing middle-aged and then old.'

'I shall be perfectly happy,' commented Betsie.

'So shall I,' said Corrie.

***

In the next few years, the ten Booms and most others in Europe became more and more concerned about what was happening in Germany. The National Socialist German Workers' Party, called Nazi for short, had once been a small, weak group, but now it had millions of members. They loved marching through the streets, singing patriotic songs and waving red and white flags, each bearing the crooked cross known as the swastika, and they were all devoted to their leader – a rather ordinary-looking man with a stubby moustache. His name was Adolf Hitler.

At the end of the First World War, he had been, apparently, just another wounded soldier. But inside him burnt twin fires of rage and ambition – rage against those he blamed for Germany's defeat, and ambition for personal and national power. Steadily he climbed the ladder of success – from leader of the Nazi party, to chancellor of Germany, then president, and finally supreme commander with the powers of a dictator.

Already he had built up a large army and navy and now ugly stories were spreading about his treatment of communists and Jews. There were tales of beatings, torture and even murder. But they couldn't be true. Could they?

DARK SHADOWS

A cruel wind blew round Haarlem one wintry night. In the morning Corrie opened the shutters and noticed treacherous patches of ice glittering on roads and pavements.

She was sitting in the dining room a little later when the door burst open and in stumbled the old clockmaker who had been working at the shop for years.

'Christoffels.' she exclaimed, for the little man who was normally very dignified, was now hatless, his coat was torn and there was blood on his cheek.

'Come and sit down, old friend,' said Casper, guiding him to a chair, 'and tell us what happened.'

'My hat fell off in the alley,' mumbled Christoffels, and said no more.

'I'll go and get it,' said Corrie, partly hoping to find out the truth and partly afraid of it.

The cold bit into her as she stepped out into the street. In the alley was a little knot of people with angry indignant faces turned towards a tall young man.

With a sinking heart, Corrie recognised him – Otto, the German apprentice, who had been working with them for some months now. His face was as hard and cold as ice.

She walked over and said, 'What happened?'

'You may well ask,' answered a man. 'I saw it all. The old man was walking along minding his own business, when he' – pointing at Otto – 'deliberately shoved him into the wall and ground his face against the bricks.'

Anger, shock and horror swept through Corrie, followed by a feeling of bewildered sadness.

'Oh, Otto, how could you?' she said. He made no reply but his eyes sent a shiver of fear through her. She stooped to pick up Christoffel's hat, then went back to the shop. Otto followed, his head held high, his footsteps firm.

'Wait here, please,' Corrie said to Otto, as he stepped into the shop after her. Then she went through the workroom and hall and over to the dining room. Betsie met her at the door and spoke to her in a low voice.

'I've cleaned the blood off his face and given him a cup of coffee, but he hasn't said anything, not even to Father. Do you know what happened, Corrie?'

'I'm afraid I do,' she answered sadly. 'Ask Father to come into the hall and I'll tell you both about it.'

Casper and Betsie were looking sad and dismayed by the time Corrie finished speaking.

'We should have listened to Willem,' she added. 'He warned us about this.'

'I kept hoping that Otto would be attracted by our way of life, and change,' said her father.

'Well, I'm afraid he hasn't, Father,' said Corrie. 'First he refuses to come to morning and evening prayers and we ignore that. Then he starts treating Christoffels badly in little ways and we turn a blind eye. But now we shall have to do something.'

'I shall go and reason with him at once,' her father said.

'Oh yes, Father, do,' said Betsie. 'He might see how wrong he's been.'

Corrie shook her head and remarked gravely, 'I doubt it.'

Casper went into the shop. He only stayed there a short time, but his daughters thought he looked years older when he came out again.

'I have had to ask Otto to leave,' he said, shaking his head as if he couldn't quite believe what had happened, for this was the first time he had ever had to sack an employee. 'He has shown no remorse whatsoever.'

Betsie put an arm round her father's shoulders while Corrie went into the shop. Otto was gathering up his things. When he'd collected them he opened the door and strode out. In closing it, he turned his face towards her again for a few seconds. It was full of scorn.

The ten Booms and Christoffels went about their work, knowing that a shadow of a very great evil had fallen on them.

'Just think,' said Corrie, 'there are thousands of young people in Germany, and some even in Holland, who are like Otto – dedicated Nazis, trained to believe that the sick, the old and the weak are just a nuisance.'

'But he's always so polite to me,' said Casper. 'And I'm older than Christoffels.'

'Yes, but you are in authority. The Nazis are taught to respect authority, and even blindly obey it, Willem says,' Corrie reminded him. 'What will all this lead to?'

'It has to lead to war,' said Willem gravely. The ten Booms, like most other families in Europe, had just heard the horrifying news of Germany's invasion of Poland.

Winter melted into spring, and spring into summer. The corn ripened and was harvested and now the countryside was getting ready for the calm of autumn. But the people of Europe were far from calm, as they huddled round their wireless sets, waiting to learn of Hitler's next move. For three years he had been building up his army, navy and air force. Then he'd taken over Czechoslovakia and made treaties with Italy and Russia. Now German troops were swarming into Poland while her cities were being bombed from the air.

'Is there no way out?' asked Betsie.

Willem shook his head and said, 'As Poland's ally, Britain will have to declare war on Germany.'

'But only twenty years ago the leaders of the nations met to stop this kind of war ever breaking out again,' Corrie pointed out. 'Agreements were drawn up and signed by all the nations concerned.'

'Agreements only work between men of honour,' said Father.

'Exactly,' said Willem. 'And Hitler has none.'

'Do you think it will be possible for Holland to stay neutral this time?' asked Betsie. Her brother shook his head.

'Hitler is interested in one thing – to bring power and glory to the great German nation – and to himself, of course. If Holland can be useful to him, then he'll try to take her – neutral or not.'

Three days later Britain declared war on Germany, but by then Poland had no air force left and only a weakened army. It was not long before she was defeated and under German control.

While Britain and Germany planned war against each other, British troops, which had been rushed to the trenches in France and Belgium, waited – tense and ready for action. By spring of the following year, they were still waiting.

***

Corrie woke up in a panic. It was very early, but the noise was terrifying, deafening. The truth hit her with sickening force. Germany had invaded Holland.

She got out of bed and crept down to Betsie's room. Her sister was awake and the two women sat on the bed, clinging to one another as bombs exploded not far away and a strange light flared in the sky.

'They must be bombing the little airport near Haarlem,' said Corrie.

'Let's pray,' said Betsie. They tiptoed into the parlour and knelt side-by-side.

'Oh, Lord, bless our Queen Wilhelmina, we pray, and give the Dutch government wisdom, and comfort the injured and dying,' prayed Corrie.

'We ask that you will have mercy on the Germans,' said Betsie.

Corrie turned an astonished face towards her sister but she continued calmly, 'We know that the men up there dropping bombs on us are in the grip of Satan's evil power and need your help so much.'

Corrie turned back to her own prayers, 'Lord, please listen to Betsie, for I simply cannot pray for the Germans.'

Suddenly a picture formed in her mind. Every detail was clear. She could see the market-square with St Bavo's and the Town Hall in the background. In the foreground something was moving across the cobbles. It was a wagon pulled by four black horses. And in the back of the wagon sat people she recognised. She was there, and so were Father and Betsie and Willem and Nollie with her clever musical son, Peter. They were all being taken to a place they didn't want to go to …

She shuddered and said, 'I've had a kind of nightmare. It was horrible, Betsie.'

'Let's go and make some coffee,' her sister suggested. They sat by the stove, sipping hot drinks, while Corrie described what she had seen. Then she asked,

'What does it mean?'

'I don't know,' answered Betsie, 'but perhaps God is showing you a bit of the future so that when it comes, you will know it was all in his plan.'

***

The flat, far-flung Dutch countryside on which thousands of German paratroopers landed, and across which thousands of German tanks roared, was a symphony of spring flowers against a background of all shades of green, intersected by mirror-smooth waterways and cupped by the wide dome of the sky.

Holland fought back bravely but her leaders had not been expecting an air attack and the Dutch air force and army were small and inexperienced.

To slow down the invaders, the people opened their dykes and flooded wide stretches of land. Hitler wanted the conquest of this little country speeded up rather than delayed. He sent a message to its leaders: 'Surrender or I will destroy Rotterdam'.

While talks were in progress, the bombing began, and soon Holland's greatest port was in ruins. When Hitler threatened to do the same thing to Utrecht, the Dutch government surrendered. The conquest of Holland had taken five days.

'What will happen now – with our Queen and government in England?' Corrie asked. Like many others, she had been upset to hear that Holland's leaders had left the country. It seemed like desertion on their part.

'I'm sure they'll go on doing their best for us,' said Father, and Willem nodded, 'I think we can be thankful that our Dutch soldiers managed to save The Hague just long enough to give our Queen and ministers a chance to escape. They can do far more good for our country from abroad than if they had stayed here and been under Nazi control.'

'Perhaps things will not be so bad,' said Betsie. 'The German soldiers seem very well-disciplined.'

'Oh, they will be bad, all right,' replied Willem. 'Especially for our Jewish friends.' Father's face grew sad as he thought of the wholesalers of Amsterdam who supplied him with parts for his watches, the rabbi in Haarlem, and many other Jews he counted among his friends or had done business with over the years. Corrie, sensing his thoughts, felt sad too. She turned to Willem, who long before this had written a paper warning people about what he had foreseen would happen, and asked, 'What is it exactly that Hitler's got against the Jews?'

'Who knows for sure,' answered her brother. 'But I believe they're his scapegoats. He needed someone to blame for Germany's defeat in the First World War, and, for some reason, picked on the Jews.'

'But why does he hate the old and weak?' asked Betsie. 'They can't harm him.'

'Perhaps not,' replied Willem. 'But they get in the way of his greatest ambition – to create a race of strong, intelligent pure Germans, who will one day rule Europe with him.'

'But that's impossible.' exclaimed Corrie.

'Let's pray that you are right,' said her father.

***

For once the little watch shop was making quite a profit. Well-paid German soldiers made good customers. And they were, as Betsie had said, well-disciplined – at first. But their presence upset the Dutch people, reminding them that they were no longer free and independent.

More and more German orders had to be obeyed.

'Everyone must carry identity cards.'

'Everyone must be off the streets by ten ... eight ... six o'clock.'

'It is forbidden to use the Dutch flag or sing the Dutch national anthem.'

'All Jews must wear a six-pointed star at all times.'

'No one is permitted to listen to the BBC news. All wireless sets must be handed in.'

'I'll hand in one wireless set and keep the other,' said Corrie. 'We must know what is happening, and it's no use relying on the newspapers for real news these days.'

The Nazis had taken over all Dutch newspapers and filled them with Hitler's speeches and stories of great German victories. And, for the first year and a half of the war, there had been plenty of German victories to report on, as Poland, Holland, Belgium and France were conquered and occupied one by one, and the British troops were driven north to Dunkirk. The soldiers had been rescued and taken home from there, though their valuable equipment had had to be left behind.

But since then, things hadn't been going quite so well for Germany. She had attacked Russia and been amazed at the way that country was fighting back, and Britain seemed to be winning the battle in the air. The newspapers wrote their own versions of these happenings, but most of the people learned the truth from their secret wireless sets.

***

'Oh, look, Father, another restaurant closed to Jews,' said Corrie sadly, pointing to the sign in the window which read: 'No Jews served here'.

It was a mild December day. Rain had fallen earlier and the streets were still wet, with a few puddles here and there. Holland had been under German rule for nineteen months.

Casper was looking old and frail now. He stared at the notice, shaking his head and saying, 'Willem was right. What happened in Germany is now happening here. The Jews are having everything taken from them – their homes, their jobs, and all their rights.'

Corrie sighed and they moved on slowly.

'Poor Father,' she thought. 'These walks are no longer the pleasure they used to be for him. How he loved stopping to greet friends and neighbours and to share the latest news.' But nowadays, people were anxious to be off the streets, away from the arrogant German soldiers.

And today the market-square was full of them, Corrie noticed. 'What is going on?' she wondered.

She guided her father towards the square and behind the lines of soldiers until they could see what was happening.

There was a truck parked in front of the fish market. Climbing meekly, numbly, into it were men, women and children, all wearing the bright yellow star.

'Where will they be taken?' she wondered. The official German answer was: 'To work camps'. But there were rumours about other sorts of camps, which the Germans had built in Poland and elsewhere – concentration camps. Would these poor people end up in one of these?

She shuddered. The truck moved off, the soldiers marched away and Corrie and her father turned homeward.

'Poor Germany,' said Casper suddenly. 'Her people will pay bitterly for what they are doing to the Jews.'

They walked on in silence. A sodden newspaper lay in Corrie's path and she stepped over it, brightening a little at the thought. 'It's probably still full of German victories, when the truth is that things are going badly for them now.'

The Russians, who had been fighting bravely since June, had counter-attacked.

A day later, Japan had come into the war on the side of Germany, but her attack on Pearl Harbour had brought the Americans in, so now Britain had a new, rich powerful ally. Britain, Russia and America – together they would win, surely.

'Let it be soon, dear Lord,' she prayed.

They had reached the house. She helped her father inside and closed the door thankfully behind them.

⏱ RESISTANCE LEADER ⏱

Corrie was sitting in the train for Hilversum. The compartment was very full and very dirty and there seemed to be a lot of stopping, starting and waiting.

'Once upon a time, before the occupation,' she thought, 'Dutch trains were a pleasure to ride in, but not any more.'

She looked out of the window and a scene in a nearby street caught her eye before the train passed on. A bicycle blockade. Some soldiers had set up a road block and were confiscating all cycles as they reached that point.

'Poor Holland.' thought Corrie. For two years the Nazis had been stripping her of young men, food, clothes, weapons and anything else that was wanted back in Germany.

She turned her head away, and tried to collect her thoughts. So much had happened in the last few days and she needed to see Willem urgently.

Three Jews had come knocking at their door, asking for help and they had taken them in. As far as Corrie was concerned, they were the answer to her prayer of a few weeks earlier.

'Lord, your people, the Jews, are suffering terribly. If I can help them in any way, at any time, please use me.'

And now it looked as though God wanted to use her. But taking in refugees was one thing. What to do with them next was quite another. Willem would help her, she was sure.

Six months earlier, Mr Weils, the owner of the fur-shop opposite had been thrown out into the street by German soldiers, and she and Betsie had taken him in for the night, but it had been Willem who had arranged for him to be moved to a place of safety in the country.

The train arrived at last, and Corrie made her way towards the nursing home. It was a beautiful spring day, but the brightness all around was not reflected in people's expressions. Many faces looked tense, many eyes frightened.

She went up to the big house and rang the bell. Tine opened the door and gave her a warm welcome. Corrie lingered to talk to her nephews and nieces, and then she was alone with Willem.

'You look tired. You're not sick, are you?' she asked her brother, noticing his drawn face. He shook his head.

'I'm all right,' he said. 'We're just a bit overcrowded and busy at the moment. More and more Jews are arriving.'

'That's what I came to see you about,' said Corrie, eagerly. 'We have three homeless Jews staying with us. It's dangerous for them to be so near the police station, so I wondered whether you would be able to arrange for them to go somewhere safer, like you did for the Weils.'

She stopped in surprise for Willem was shaking his head.

'Corrie, I wish I could help you, but I can't,' he said, wearily. 'I have enough to do running things here. And I'm being watched all the time now.'

'I see,' said Corrie. 'Well, what am I to do with these poor people? And there'll be more arriving – I'm sure of that.'

'There's only one thing to do,' said Willem. 'You'll have to head up a group in Haarlem.'

Corrie stared at him.

'A group? What do you mean?'

'A resistance group of underground workers,' said her brother, slowly. Corrie's eyes grew rounder than ever.

'You don't mean to say that you are ...' she began.

'A member of the Dutch underground?' Willem finished for her. 'Well, of course I am, Corrie. How else could I help and hide Jews in the way that I do? But you needn't look so shocked. I don't know what you've heard about the underground, but we don't all blow up bridges and kill people.'

'What do you do, then?' asked Corrie, still reeling, although it had crossed her mind before that Willem and his tall, blond son, Kik, were involved in a secret group of some kind.

'Well, as you know, Jews are not allowed ration cards, permits of one kind or another, and so on, so we supply them with whatever they need,' Willem answered.

'How?' Corrie demanded.

'Oh, in all sorts of ways,' said her brother, casually. 'By making contacts with sympathetic people in shops, hospitals, business, government departments, or raiding food offices, or forging papers – that sort of thing.'

'And you think I could do all that?'

'Well, couldn't you?' probed Willem, looking straight into her eyes. She was silent, and he went on, 'Corrie, the disease of Nazism is spreading fast. People all over Holland are joining the Dutch Nazi Movement and helping the Germans. We must do something to try and stop what is happening. Joining the resistance is one way of doing this. We can't resist openly, so we have to do it secretly. Think about it, Corrie.'

Corrie's mind was in a whirl as she travelled home. What Willem had suggested was impossible.

Or was it?

'We have friends all over Haarlem,' Corrie realised, slowly. 'There are Father's watchmaking friends as well as all the people my parents have been so good to.'

'Dear Lord,' she prayed, 'if you want me to do this work, please give me the strength and the helpers and contacts I need.'

Suddenly she thought of someone – the father of one of the children in her class of retarded children. Once a meter reader for the electricity company, he now worked in a food office. 'Would this man, Fred Koornstra, help me to get extra ration cards?' she wondered.

And then there was that friend at the telephone exchange. Would he be able to reconnect their telephone secretly?

One after another, faces and names came into her mind – a young man who might be a courier, a nurse who might help with medicines, a shopkeeper who might be willing to use his van …

Corrie and Betsie talked and prayed and planned. As more and more Jews arrived, Betsie made up beds and cooked more food, while Corrie and her growing team of helpers set about finding safe places for them to go, and organising transport and ration cards.

***

'Betsie, it was wonderful. There were lawyers, architects, postmen, musicians, factory workers, members of the Dutch police – people from every sort of job, all working for the resistance. I felt so ordinary among them, but everyone was so kind.'

Corrie was sitting on Betsie's bed late one night, describing her first meeting with other leaders of the Dutch resistance movement. Earlier that evening, but after curfew time, Kik had called for her and together they had cycled through the dark streets at a terrifying speed, as far as Corrie was concerned, to the house where all these people had gathered.

'What do they do?' asked Betsie.

'Their main work is keeping in touch with Britain and the free Dutch forces outside Holland', said Corrie. 'And helping the British and Americans inside Holland, of course. Remember that plane which crashed near Zandvoort? Well, some members of the resistance rescued the crew and got them all safely to the North Sea coast. They have a secret route all worked out.'

'What brave people.' said Betsie. 'Do we know any of them?'

'They're all surnamed Smit.' answered Corrie, laughing. 'And one of them is coming round here soon. They think we need a secret room and "Mr Smit" is going to supervise the work.'

'Goodness. The house is full of secret places already.' Betsie exclaimed, thinking of the hollow spaces under the stairs – one of which held their wireless set, another some money and jewellery, and a third the hundred ration cards which Fred Koornstra had willingly supplied.

A few days later, 'Mr Smit' arrived. Corrie accompanied him as he walked all round the house – tapping walls and floors, staring at ceilings, calculating ... Finally he reached the top floor and seemed delighted with the little rooms up there. After more tapping and measuring he went into one room and announced, 'We will build a secret room here. It's perfect.'

'It's my bedroom.' said Corrie, in mock protest. More visitors called and produced bricks, nails, hammers, cement ... Casper shook each new arrival warmly by the hand, but after meeting several, he exclaimed in mild surprise, 'So many Smits. It's quite amazing.'

After six days, Corrie, Betsie and Casper stared around the room in astonishment.

'It looks just the same as before.' exclaimed Betsie.

'Exactly.' said Corrie. 'No one would ever know this was a new wall.' She ran her hand over the apparently weathered surface.

Mr Smit gave the same wall a hard tap.

'Hear that?' he asked with a touch of pride in his voice. 'Solid brick, just like the other three walls. If I'd used wood, it would have sounded hollow.'

'Remarkable, Mr Smit,' said Casper. 'And all done so quickly too.'

Mr Smit smiled, then went towards some shelves built along the new wall. They, too, looked well weathered. He put his hand under the bottom shelf and slid back a panel.

'After you,' he said to Corrie and Betsie. They went across, stooped to crawl through the opening, and then stood up and looked round the tiny square room. Mr Smit followed.

'It's wonderful.' said Betsie.

'It'll hold eight people standing up,' said Mr Smit. 'And there's an air vent here, let in from the outer wall. You must put a mattress on the floor and keep water and biscuits here all the time.'

They went back through the opening and rejoined Casper who had chosen to remain in Corrie's bedroom.

'The next thing to do,' said Mr Smit, 'is to have an alarm system. Wire the house up and put buttons in almost all the rooms so that you can buzz a warning to anyone in the house. And make the guests practise disappearing into the secret room. Do it over and over again, until they can get inside, with all their belongings, in under a minute.'

'One of my helpers, Leonard, is a handy man,' said Corrie. 'I think he would do the wiring for us. And we'll start the drills right away. But under a minute – that sounds impossible.'

From summer onwards, the refugees kept arriving and the little house was a centre of underground activity. Corrie threw herself enthusiastically into her new work …

***

Father was working in the shop and Betsie was trying to help him and supervise what was going on in the kitchen, where some Jewish guests, and a couple of Corrie's team, were peeling potatoes for the twelve people who would be sharing meals round the oval dining room table that day.

Upstairs in her room, Corrie had a pile of papers in front of her and a stream of people to attend to.

A young man entered, saying, 'I met Fred in his meter man uniform on his way out, and he said to tell you that he's just put two dozen ration cards in the usual place.'

'Thank you, Nils,' said Corrie. 'We need five of those right away. Are you free to take them round to this address?' She held up a piece of paper. Nils stared at it for a moment, said, 'Right, I'll remember that,' and went out.

A second man entered.

'Good news, Corrie,' he said. 'I have another family willing to take up to three Jews. I think they're safe.'

'I trust your judgement, Hank,' replied Corrie. 'As it happens, we have two new Jews here – they arrived last night. Perhaps you'd like to meet them and then make the arrangements. They're in the kitchen. If you can get transport for tonight, that would be good – we're over-full here at the moment.'

'I'll do my best,' Hank replied, as he left.

'Anything for me?' asked a young woman, entering. Corrie smiled at her sensitive, eager face. How she loved these courageous helpers of hers.

'I have three addresses here. Would you check them out for me, Mary? Make sure none of them have any Dutch Nazis living next door, or anything like that.'

'Will do,' said Mary. She took the list and studied it for a moment or two before leaving.

Corrie bent to her paperwork for a while.

Two more people came in, one of whom she knew. 'Hullo, Peter,' she said.

'Hullo,' he replied. 'This is Kurt. He's a German soldier, but he can't bear to work for the Nazis any longer. I'm sure we can trust him.'

Corrie gave the stranger a long, hard look and saw a very young face with honest, troubled blue eyes.

'Please believe me, Miss ten Boom,' he said. 'I have been wanting to leave the army for a long time now and looking for a way out.'

'All right, Kurt,' said Corrie, smiling. 'We can certainly use your uniform, so please would you hand that over to our boys, and anything else that might be useful to us, when our friends come for you? We have a farm where you will meet several others who have made the same choice as you.' She turned back to Peter and said, 'Can I leave you to arrange all the details?'

A few more moments of talk, and they left as Betsie entered with a cup of tea and a note. 'Someone called at the front door with it,' she explained, handing the paper over.

'Thank you, Betsie,' said Corrie. She swallowed a mouthful of tea, then opened the note. A frown creased her forehead as she read it.

'Is anything wrong?' asked Betsie, and Corrie nodded.

'A Jewish orphanage is to be closed down. We're going to have to rescue the babies straight away.' She sat back and closed her eyes, praying and planning.

'Let me know if I can do anything,' said Betsie quietly as she left the room.

'Now if some of our boys dressed up in Nazi uniforms,' Corrie was thinking, 'they could go round to the orphanage and demand the babies. Then we could take them to different homes. Surely no one will be able to resist a baby on their doorstep if they're told that unless they take them in, they will be killed ...'

Two more young men arrived and Corrie sat up and said briskly, 'Just the people I wanted. Leonard, could you please get seven of our boys round here right away. Use the secret phone and the usual code. And Harry – could you arrange some transport? A Jew has to be moved from a hut on a tennis court before six o'clock this evening, when people will start arriving to play ...'

The busy day flew by, with short breaks for meals. In the evening, Corrie closed her files and went down to the dining room. Betsie, Casper and the seven people staying at the house were already there.

'Ah, Corrie, I'm so glad you're going to join us this evening,' said Casper, notebook in hand. At eighty-four he was still keen to learn.

'I never miss Mary's Italian class if I can help it,' Corrie answered with a smile as she sat down. Mary was the oldest of their guests and suffered from asthma. She now started the class.

There was a relaxed atmosphere. Corrie tried to forget the pressures of the day and concentrate on language study, but she found herself looking round at her 'family' and wondering how much longer things could go on as they had been doing. Surely with all the comings and goings, and the noise, people would begin to suspect that one old watchmaker and his two unmarried daughters were not the only occupants of the corner house.

And then what would happen to Father, Betsie, and herself and those sharing their home? While many came and went, there were always at least seven people staying there – some of them Jews, and the rest underground workers.

She looked fondly at them – Eusie, who gave Hebrew lessons, and discussed the Old Testament with Father; Mary, taking the class; Thea, who played the piano beautifully; Leonard, the handyman and violinist, who was taking his turn at supplying light by pedalling furiously on her bike so that the headlamp glowed ...

'All of us are in great danger,' thought Corrie. 'And yet there is a happy atmosphere in this crowded home. It is the Lord's doing. He gives us his peace and joy and guides us step by step.'

The evening passed pleasantly. Father led family prayers and went to bed. Soon the others followed. Only Corrie lingered. She was tired, but there was one more thing to be done before she went to bed tonight.

Slowly, she walked round the house, locking the doors, checking the windows, waiting till all was quiet upstairs. Then she went into the hall and put her thumb on a button for a second. Afterwards, she stood still, looking at her watch and listening intently.

A creak, a footstep, a cough.

'Not bad,' she thought, picturing the guests snatching up sheets and belongings, folding blankets, turning mattresses, going into her bedroom, squeezing into the space behind the false wall.

She started to climb the stairs, smiling at a childhood memory of hide-and-seek and herself shouting, 'Coming – ready or not.'

She went into one room after another, searching for tell-tale objects, touching each mattress. At last she reached her own room. From behind the wall Mary's wheeze could be heard clearly enough. If this had been a real raid, she'd have given the hiding place away. But those sharing the little room with her had all voted that she be allowed to stay.

'You can all come out now.' Corrie called. The panel slid back and out they crawled, laughing and joking.

'Better than last time,' said Corrie. 'But there was one warm mattress and a collar stud. And you took two minutes. Still I think you deserve your cream buns.'

'Good old Aunt Corrie.' they chorused and flopped down on the bedroom floor, to eat and chatter and laugh, like children at a midnight feast. But, deep down, each one knew that this wasn't just a game ...

Summer yielded to autumn and autumn to winter. Underground workers continued to slip in and out of the corner house. Jews came and went. Corrie, Betsie, and their seven permanent guests shared in the life of the home, helping with the chores, joining in with daily prayers, and taking part in the evening activities of singing and making music, reading books and plays, talking and learning together.

In bleak, misty November, there was rejoicing at the news that the British were driving the Germans back from Egypt, and that British and American troops had landed in French North Africa. But in Holland, and the rest of Nazi-controlled Europe, life was harsh – with less food, less fuel, less chance of escape for young men and Jews, and more rules, restrictions and Gestapo raids.

Corrie was busier than ever and the house was always full ... There were twelve people sitting round the oval dining room table when the shop bell rang. The talking stopped abruptly. It was past curfew time, so the caller must be pretty desperate or else ...

Corrie got up and went to the door, calling, 'Who's there?'

In German a voice replied, 'An old friend.'

Corrie unlocked the door and a man in uniform pushed his way inside.

'Captain Altschuler,' he announced. 'You remember me.'

It was Otto.

'Well, aren't you going to ask me in to talk about old times?' he said with a sneer.

'He hasn't changed,' thought Corrie. 'The same arrogance.' But she forced herself to smile and answer, 'Yes, of course,' while desperately wondering how she could reach a buzzer and delay him.

She started to talk about anything that came into her head. Coming level with the counter in the shop, she paused and slid a hand along underneath the top, groping for the button. She found it at last.

'What was that noise?' snapped Otto, stiffening.

'I didn't hear anything,' said Corrie. 'You know, Otto, er, Captain Altschuler, Christoffels died last winter. It was so cold ...'

'Huh. That old man. And the Bible reader?'

'My father is keeping quite well, thank you.'

All too soon they reached the dining room.

'Father, Betsie, you'll never guess who's here?' Corrie called out, playing for time, but Otto stretched out a long arm and pushed the door wide open.

Corrie's heart thumped wildly. Then she saw the table and almost gasped, her relief was so great.

It was set for three. Father and Betsie looked calmly up from their meal to greet Otto politely.

He pulled out a chair, sat down and crowed, 'Well, I said that Germany would triumph, and I was right.' Betsie handed him a cup of tea and he sipped it and went on talking of German might and victories.

After what seemed a long time but was only fifteen minutes, he left, and his listeners breathed sighs of relief.

'We can't let the others out yet,' said Corrie. 'Just in case Otto comes back.'

'That poor, foolish boy.' said Casper, shaking his head.

'How can he believe that Germany is still winning?' asked Betsie. 'Doesn't he know that her armies have been pushed out of North Africa, and that the Russians, British and Americans are advancing east and south all the time now?'

'Probably not,' said Corrie. 'He calls himself a captain, but he's not, and he's probably been told a pack of lies by his superiors.'

After half an hour she thought it was safe to go upstairs and call, 'All clear'. Nine cramped people emerged to stretch their legs and find out what had happened.

'You were perfect.' Corrie told them. 'I didn't hear a sound.'

***

'It's getting almost impossible to find safe places,' Corrie told Betsie one evening. For nearly two years she and her team of eighty workers had been running a resistance group which had helped hundreds of Jews. But things were getting more difficult and dangerous all the time.

'Should we stop, Betsie?' she asked. 'What do you think?'

'How can we stop when the needs are greater than ever?' replied Betsie.

'That's what I feel,' said Corrie. She sighed, and added, 'Ironic – isn't it? – that as the news from the war gets better and better, things in occupied Europe become worse and worse.'

Betsie nodded, and they fell silent, lost in sad thoughts.

Corrie grieved for her fellow-Netherlanders, forced to eat tulip bulbs and rotten potatoes to stave off starvation these days. It hurt her deeply to think of thousands of Dutch lads working in weapons factories in Germany. It tore her apart to know that millions of Jews were in concentration camps, along with the sick, the old and the handicapped.

Betsie was right. Of course they must go on, in God's strength, with his love, doing what they could to help those who were suffering.

But the price might be very high, for them all. Peter had been kept in prison two months for playing the Dutch national anthem after a church service. Nollie had spent seven weeks in a cell for having a Jewess in her home. So if Otto or any of his colleagues should burst into the house and catch them red-handed, there was no telling what might happen.

'But, Lord, you are in control. Help us to follow you step by step,' she prayed.

⏱ THE TRAP ⏱

Corrie sat up in bed trying to sort out the papers in front of her. There was so much to do. A Jew had died and a secret burial would need to be arranged for him. New hiding places were wanted. She must contact her medical friends and try to arrange a bed for a pregnant Jewish woman.

But it was no use. She simply couldn't concentrate. Even a leader of the Dutch resistance couldn't resist a bad attack of flu. She pushed her papers into her case and lay back on the pillows. One moment, she was on fire, the next icy-cold.

Before dozing off, she remembered the caller they had had earlier on.

'He insists in seeing you,' Betsie had said. So Corrie had had to force her aching body out of bed and down the stairs.

'Please help me,' the man had begged. 'We have been hiding Jews and my wife has been arrested. We must rescue her before she is taken to Amsterdam for questioning. If she talks, many lives will be in danger.'

'How can I help you?' Corrie had asked, trying to sound surprised.

He answered, 'We need money. There is a policeman who will help us if we pay him. We know you have contacts and could raise the money.'

Corrie's eyes had been watering and her head pounding.

'All right,' she'd said, and quickly made the necessary arrangements before going back to bed.

Now, on the edge of sleep, she thought, 'If only he'd looked me straight in the eye ...'

She woke with a start. People were scurrying across her room – four Jewish refugees and two underground workers.

'What a funny time to be having a practice drill,' she thought. Then her eyes focused on Eusie's face and the truth stabbed her. This was not a practice. It was the real thing. Loud voices and the stamping of booted feet told her that the Germans were in the house at this very moment. At least someone had managed to press a buzzer, but would their guests be able to hide in time?

Mary was now squeezing herself through the opening in the wall, followed by a member of the resistance, so now six people were safely inside with their things. With Leonard away, that was everyone hidden who ought to be.

'Oh no.' thought Corrie – as the sound of poor asthmatic Mary's wheezing could be heard through the wall. Desperately she prayed, 'Lord, please stop Mary's wheezing right now.'

Not another sound came from behind the false wall.

'My case.' was Corrie's next thought. The Germans mustn't find the papers in there, with names, addresses and details of the group.

She shot out of bed, snatched up the case, and hurried to the secret panel. In seconds she had opened it, flung the case inside, closed it, and dived back into bed – just in time.

The Germans were coming up the stairs. One burst into her room, saw her and snapped, 'Your identity card.' Corrie took the paper from the little pouch she wore round her neck and handed it to him. He stared at it, then turned a sneering face towards her and said, 'So you're the ringleader. Get dressed.'

Groggily, Corrie got up and reached for her clothes.

'Where are you hiding your Jews?'

'I'm not going to tell you.'

'Don't worry. We'll find them, even if we have to watch the house till they all turn to mummies.' he said with a sadistic smile.

Corrie finished dressing. All she needed now was what she thought of as her 'prison case'. In it were a Bible, washing things, a few clothes and a bottle of vitamins. She took a step towards it, then stopped, realising where it was – right in front of the trap door. She couldn't, she mustn't go over there. But how could she face prison without a Bible, and the other little comforts?

'Dear Lord, help me not to be selfish,' she prayed. For what seemed a long time, but could only have been a few seconds, a struggle went on inside her. Then she walked straight out of her room and down the stairs.

The scene in the dining room made her heart turn over. Nollie, Willem, Peter, and many of their friends, were sitting or standing against the walls, guarded by armed German police – the Gestapo.

'It would be a morning when Willem was holding one of his Bible study groups here and Nollie had called round.' thought Corrie, sadly.

'In there,' barked the Gestapo leader, jerking his chin in the direction of the shop. Corrie went in and sat facing him. She could hear a lot of banging, shouting and tramping about going on above her and thought, 'They haven't found the secret room. Dear "Mr Smit" did his work well.'

'Take off your glasses.' the man growled.

Corrie did so.

'Where are you hiding your Jews?' The question was accompanied by a stinging slap across her face. She flinched, but did not answer. More questions and more slaps followed until she felt she couldn't bear it any longer.

Suddenly she remembered the day the headmaster had slapped her face, and how she'd found comfort in her father's arms.

'Lord Jesus, protect me.' she cried out. For a second, time seemed to stand still. Then the man spoke in a menacing voice.

'Mention that name again and I'll kill you.'

But there were no more slaps.

She was dismissed – without her glasses – and Betsie was taken through for questioning. Corrie sat on a chair in the dining room looking round at the faces of her family and friends. She felt sick, bruised and sad. At the sight of her father's frail form, she rose to go across and put her arms round him. But a guard pushed her down again and made her sit facing the wall.

Betsie came back in, her cheeks very red.

'Oh, my poor, gentle sister.' thought Corrie. 'But at least they haven't found the secret room.'

Other hidden things had been discovered though – money, the wireless, watches, bits of jewellery. Most of these had disappeared into the pockets of the Gestapo officers.

The doorbell rang and Corrie's heart sank, as she thought, 'It'll be one of our friends with a message and whoever it is will fall straight into the trap.'

The Gestapo man who went to the door was dressed in ordinary clothes, so the woman standing outside suspected nothing. Besides, the wooden triangle was sitting in the window – and that meant it was safe to call.

Helplessly, Corrie listened to her friend saying, 'Uncle Herman has been caught. Will you pass on the message?'

'Yes, of course,' was the smooth reply. 'Who should I give a message to?'

'Oh, the people who come here,' answered the woman. Too late she saw the vicious smile and knew that she had blundered. The man grabbed her and took her through to the dining room. Corrie saw her shocked face as she came in.

A sudden quiet but unmistakable ringing made her jump.

'Oh, no, not our secret phone.' she thought, but a man ordered her to answer it. Corrie walked towards it, desperately trying to think of a way of warning the caller. She picked up the receiver and said, 'The ten Boom home.' in what she hoped was a strange voice, but the person on the other end of the line was too anxious to deliver his message to notice.

'They've got Herman. Be careful.'

'Yes, thank you. Goodbye,' she answered. With the armed Gestapo officer standing over her, she dared not say more.

Time dragged by. There were more phone calls, but at last someone understood Corrie's hidden message, and the line went dead.

Betsie spoke in her calm voice.

'It's time to eat. May I please cut some bread and offer it round?' An officer nodded curtly.

Corrie, facing the wall, could only watch her sister's graceful movements some of the time. She was passing the fireplace now, and seemed to be pausing, pointing at something – a tile.

Corrie understood. She knew what was written there: 'Jesus is victor'.

'He certainly is,' said the quiet voice of her father.

Corrie was suddenly filled with joy. Jesus was here. Jesus was in control.

The searchers came down, furious at not having found the secret room.

'Take the prisoners to the police station,' said the Gestapo leader.

Everyone left the dining room. Corrie exchanged loving glances with her family and friends as they filed out. She waited for her father and then walked beside him, out of their home and along the street, towards the tall, red-brick building nearby.

The cold February air started her shivering again. She put an arm round her father and prayed, 'Dear God, protect this wonderful old man.'

They were taken inside the gloomy police building and along to the gym.

'Sit down.' came the order. Corrie led her father to a mat and helped him settle down on it. She looked round, counting. Thirty-five people she knew, and a few others she didn't.

'The thing to do is to get our group together and try to sort out what we'll say when we're questioned,' she thought. Her nephew Peter came quietly across to her and whispered, 'Be very careful, Auntie. There is a German spy among us.'

'Well, Lord,' thought Corrie, 'we shall just have to trust you for the words to speak when the time comes.'

The hours crawled by. Corrie shivered and sweated – and stayed close to her father. He was beginning to droop now.

'Ah, good.' she thought, seeing rolls being brought in. They tasted delicious. Then they were left to sit around and wait.

'It looks as though they're going to leave us here for the night,' thought Corrie.

She looked at her watch and saw that it was well past her father's bedtime.

'Willem, will you read Psalm 91 for us?' His voice broke in on her thoughts.

'Of course, Father.'

A little group gathered round the ten Booms and listened to Willem's deep voice reading.

'I will say of the Lord, he is my refuge and my fortress: my God, in him will I trust ... Thou shalt not be afraid for the terror by night.'

The reading ended, and the old man prayed, asking for God's protection and blessing.

No one slept well on the floor of the gym. Corrie woke with a pain in her chest, and saw that her father looked very white. The prisoners dozed or talked quietly until noon. Then the soldiers took them out of the station to a waiting bus.

Betsie and Corrie supported their father between them as they stepped into the street. There were some people looking on. Corrie recognised friends and neighbours and saw the horror and pity on their faces as they watched old Casper go by – the man everyone in Haarlem loved and respected.

'The best is yet to be, Father,' Corrie whispered.

'It certainly is,' he answered.

They boarded the bus and it moved off. Corrie stared out of the window for a last glimpse of the places she loved – the streets near her home, the market-square, St Bavo's, the Town Hall ...

They faded into the distance. Now they were passing stretches of flat countryside. Today the weather was almost spring-like. The sort of day when she and her club-girls might have tramped through country lanes, laughing and chattering together.

'Where are they taking us?' she wondered. Suddenly she remembered her dream. It had come true. Only, instead of a wagon and horses, there was this bus taking Father, his four children, one of his grandchildren and many friends to a place they didn't want to go to.

The Hague, once the seat of the Dutch government, was their first stop. Weary hours of queuing and form-filling followed, with Father growing weaker and weaker, and then they boarded a truck which jolted west.

'Scheveningen,' was the whispered word passing along the truck. Corrie knew a little about this place. It was a fishing village. No doubt it had a fleet of attractive boats.

It also had a prison, a place where convicted thieves, and possibly even murderers were kept.

'Surely not there.' Corrie thought. 'Poor Father among criminals – oh no.'

But the gates of the grim stone building opened and the truck drove through.

⏱ SOLITARY IN SCHEVENINGEN ⏱

Corrie tossed and turned on the hard, iron cot, and started to cough again as the straw-dust from the mattress got into her throat. From the floor below another prisoner stirred and muttered. In her first week in this dark, airless cell, Corrie had tried to make friends with the other women, but now the days and nights were a fevered blur. Every tiny movement and every thought brought pain.

Nollie, Willem and Peter – where were they? And Betsie, with her poor health, how would she survive on gruel and coarse prison bread? And dear Father – how could anyone want to hurt him? She pictured him sitting in the prison courtyard looking dignified, but so old and frail.

'Ten Boom Cornelia,' a guard had shouted, and she'd only had time to stoop and kiss him, whispering, 'God be with you, Father.

'And with you,' he'd said. Since then her world had been this cell with its filthy blankets, grimy washbasin, sewage bucket and waste bin which had to be passed out to the heartless women guards, who banged down the food plates on the shelf in the door. The night dragged on and came to an end at last. Iron bolts rasped, doors banged open, on went the light in its naked bulb.

'Ten Boom Cornelia, get on your coat and hat,' shouted the guard. Corrie struggled out of bed and put on her things.

'Where to now?' she wondered, wearily, as she trudged down the corridor.

Fresh air at last. She stood in the courtyard breathing deeply until a fit of coughing racked her. Two other prisoners were brought out.

'They look even sicker than I feel,' thought Corrie. There was a car waiting. The three unhealthy-looking women were bundled inside, with their guards.

'Are they taking us to hospital?' Corrie wondered. In a few moments, she recognised the streets of The Hague.

The car stopped and the prisoners were taken into a huge building.

'What a depressing place.' thought Corrie, looking at the lines of pale, haggard people waiting to see the doctor. She and the other two joined the queue.

A nurse was approaching. Corrie caught her eye and asked, 'Please may I wash my hands?'

'Come with me,' she said, and led the way to the bathroom. When Corrie was inside, the nurse closed the door, put her arms round Corrie and whispered, 'Can I do anything for you – get you something, perhaps?'

Corrie had almost forgotten that people could be kind. She looked gratefully at the nurse and said promptly, 'A Bible, please.' Then added, 'And a pencil, soap, safety pins, toothbrush and a needle and thread – if you can.'

The nurse looked doubtful and replied, 'I'll try, but it won't be easy.'

Corrie came out of the bathroom and rejoined the queue feeling much brighter. At last it was her turn to see the doctor. She looked at him and thought, 'Here's someone else who cares.' He spoke to her quietly.

'I have written that you have pleurisy, so you should go to a hospital where things will be better for you.'

Corrie's smile was warm as she left him. On her way out of the room, the same nurse crossed her path, brushing up against her in passing.

Corrie slipped a hand into her pocket and felt a tiny parcel. Excitement welled up inside her, but not until she was in her cell did she open it. Her fellow-prisoners gathered round eagerly as the paper came off.

Out tumbled a pencil, soap, safety pins and ... four gospels: some of the things she had left behind in her prison case, after that sharp, inner battle.

'Thank you, Lord.' she prayed. Then she began sharing out her good things.

Her cell mates were grateful for the soap and safety pins, but they shook their heads when she held out the gospels to them.

'If we were caught with one of those, we'd get cold food for weeks.' one said.

Corrie's outing had raised her spirits, but her body was still sick, and she tossed and turned and coughed in bed that night, and the following two days and nights. Then she was called out again.

'Hospital at last,' she told herself, thinking gratefully of the doctor. She followed the guard along one corridor and then another. They were taking a long time to reach the courtyard. The guard stopped to unlock a door.

'In there,' she said. Corrie turned, and saw a cell – just like the one she had left, except that there were no other prisoners in it. Her hopes withered and died.

She stepped inside and sank on to the cot, as the guard slammed the door and slid the bolt across. An icy blast of wind blew through the tiny concrete room. Corrie shuddered and lay down, pulling one of the grey blankets round her but there was no warmth in it.

Night fell, the wind shrieked, the pipes made strange sounds and she shivered and ached and coughed.

In her heart, she kept calling out to the one she knew was with her, even here.

'Saviour, take me in your arms. Comfort me. Help me. I have no one but you.'

A feeling of peace filled her, and she slept.

Days and nights were again a blur. Bread was thrown into her cot and medicines and her warm food were brought to her by an orderly, for three days.

Bang. Corrie woke on the fourth morning with a start. A harsh voice was shouting, 'You're well enough now, so stop shamming and get your own food.' The door slammed.

Corrie got out of bed and crawled to the food-shelf. She ate what she could, then went back and lay down.

'Up, up, don't be so lazy.' shouted a guard. 'Scrub out your cell. Hurry.'

Corrie forced herself to obey. Slowly, the fever passed. Now she would be able to enjoy one thing that her cell did have – a window, with a view of the sky.

She went and stood where she could see out, and stayed there for hours, watching the changing clouds and colours, dreaming of country rambles ...

Sunlight came filtering through the bars of the window. She stood in the rays, moving as they did.

'Two luxuries in one day,' she thought. 'And now for the best one of all.' She pulled a gospel from under her mattress and opened it, thankful that at last her glasses had been returned to her.

'Let not your heart be troubled ... My peace I give to you.' Wonderful, comforting words.

'I have chosen you, and ordained you, that ye should go and bring forth fruit.'

'What kind of fruit does God want me to bring forth here in Scheveningen?' she wondered ...

***

The weeks passed. Corrie stood in the warmth and brightness of the spring sunshine, watching the clouds and dreaming of flowering cherry trees in the park, fields of brilliant flowers, sunlight on the river, gaily painted boats on the canal ... She turned away and sat down.

There was something moving across the floor of her cell. She bent to take a closer look. An ant. And another and another and another. She crouched down to watch.

'How lovely to have your company,' she whispered. 'Next time the bread comes round, I'll save you some crumbs.' Strange that she had never realised before how fascinating these creatures could be.

The sound of a key in the lock made her jump up. The door was flung open and a guard spoke. Her voice was harsh, but her words sounded promising.

'You will come with me to the shower-room.'

Corrie followed her thinking, 'What a lovely birthday present, even if it comes two days late.' Soon she would be washing away the grime of weeks and – better still – mingling with her fellow-prisoners ...

She was lying on her bed when the German officer walked in. The stars and ribbons on his uniform made bright splashes of colour in the grey cell.

'Miss ten Boom, I would like to ask you a few questions,' he said. His voice was polite.

'Is this a Nazi trick?' she wondered.

He began mentioning names and Corrie said quickly, 'These people have nothing to do with my case. Please let them go.'

He looked thoughtfully at her. 'Are you well enough to come for questioning?' he asked.

'Yes, of course,' she answered.

But it was some time before he sent for her.

'At last I am to have a hearing,' thought Corrie, following a guard through long corridors, across a courtyard and towards a hut. 'Lord, keep the door of my lips.'

As she went in, a man stood up. It was the German officer who had spoken so politely to her.

'Please sit down,' he said. Corrie did so and he went on, 'I'm Lieutenant Rahms, and I want to ask you some questions. But you look cold.' He got up and quickly rekindled the fire in the stove.

'I want to find out about raids on food offices,' he told her, when he had sat down again. 'People have been breaking in to steal ration cards and food coupons.'

Corrie breathed a sigh of relief and answered, truthfully, 'I can't help you.'

He began to speak of other things. 'What do you do in your spare time?'

'Many things, but one thing I enjoy is my class for backward children.'

'Isn't that a waste of time?'

'Jesus didn't think so. He loved and cared for the weak, helpless, lost people.'

The lieutenant gave her a long, troubled look.

He came to fetch her quite early the next morning, and they stood in the sun near the garden wall.

'I thought the fresh air would do you good,' he told her.

Corrie smiled gratefully at him, and breathed deeply. It was wonderful to be outside again. 'Lord, keep me from saying the wrong things. Show me how to speak,' she prayed – her usual prayer before any questioning sessions. Lieutenant Rahms was speaking.

'I couldn't sleep for thinking about what you told me about Jesus. Tell me more,' he said.

Corrie was thrilled. 'Jesus is the light of the world,' she said eagerly. 'He came from heaven to earth to live a perfect life, then died and rose again, so that all of us who live in darkness of sin and fear might receive his light.' She paused to look very directly into the officer's face, which was strained and tense, before asking a question.

'Is there darkness in your life, Lieutenant?'

Over the man's face came a look of utter hopelessness as he answered, 'Unbelievable darkness. I dread each new day, and worry constantly about my wife and children back home in Germany.'

He shared his fear and sadness, as Corrie thought, 'I am the prisoner, and he is part of the regime that put me here, yet there is far more joy in my life than his.'

'Jesus Christ can dispel the deepest darkness,' she told him ...

They went inside to work out her statement. She signed it and the lieutenant walked back with her to her cell. At the door, he exclaimed, 'How can you believe in a God who would let a good person like you be put in a prison like this?' Many times Corrie had asked herself this question, so she was ready with her answer.

'God never makes mistakes. There must be a good reason for his wanting me to be alone with him now.'

She added the man's name to her prayers. There was plenty of time to pray as the months passed ...

***

Prisoners were shouting.

'Whatever's happening?' Corrie wondered. Over the months, she and her neighbours had found ways of passing messages or talking quietly to one another through holes or pipes, but this was different.

She hurried to the opening in her cell door and shouted, 'What's going on?'

'It's Hitler's birthday,' someone called back. 'The guards are having a party.'

'I am Corrie ten Boom in cell 384. Does anyone know where any of my family are?' she called out, and heard the enquiry passed on. After a short while, someone said, 'There is a message for Cornelia ten Boom from Betsie. She is in cell 312 and wants to tell you that God is good.'

'How like Betsie.' thought Corrie, her eyes filling with happy tears, but she brushed them aside and called, 'This is Cornelia ten Boom in cell 384. Is there any news of Casper ten Boom?'

When the guards returned, Corrie had heard so much good news that she could have danced. Peter, Nollie and everyone else arrested in the raid on her house had been set free, except her father, Betsie and herself. Betsie was not far away, and clearly the same as ever. But there was no news of Father. Oh, how she ached to be near him ... The parcel shot through the opening in the cell door and Corrie ran to pick it up. Every other Wednesday, the prisoners received a Red Cross parcel, but this one was even more welcome. It was from Nollie. She recognised her handwriting on the outside.

Carefully, slowly, savouring every moment, she untied it and folded back the paper.

'What a feast of colour.' she thought, staring in fascination at blue and scarlet. Then she lifted up the contents and enjoyed them one by one ... a warm, blue sweater, a bright red towel, biscuits, vitamins and a needle and thread.

Dear, dear Nollie. Corrie looked again at her writing. It was Nollie's all right, but wasn't it sloping over rather heavily?

'Of course, how stupid of me.' she thought. 'It's a message.' She looked more closely and noticed that the movement of the writing was towards the stamp. Carefully she removed it and turned it over.

The writing on the back was very tiny, but she managed to make it out: 'All the watches in your cupboard are safe.'

'Oh, thank you, Lord, for this wonderful news,' Corrie prayed, knowing that the coded message meant that the six people in the secret room were free.

***

Corrie stood with the tears streaming down her face, staring through blurred eyes at a letter in her hand.

'Corrie, can you be brave?' Nollie had written. 'Father went to be with the Lord ten days after he was taken to prison.'

Great racking sobs shook her as she thought, 'No, I can't be brave. I can't bear it. I must have someone to help me.' In her desperation for human company, she called through the opening in her door. 'Help me, please. Someone come to cell 384. I have had bad news.' There were footsteps and a moment later a woman guard came in – one of the less brutal ones. 'Please stay with me, just for a few moments,' sobbed Corrie. 'My father has died.'

'Just a moment,' said the woman, and went outside. She came back with a sedative. Corrie shook her head.

'I don't want medicine – just human company.'

Awkwardly, the guard sat down. But she grew more and more uncomfortable. At last she snapped, 'It's your own fault. If you hadn't broken the law, you and your father would be together. Besides, he was an old man.'

Numbly, Corrie watched her walk to the cell door, go out and shut it behind her. Then she prayed, 'Lord, how foolish I was to expect comfort from such a person. I turn to you, now. Help me, please. Comfort me ...'

The storm of weeping passed and she lay on her bed, exhausted. Memories came flooding back.

She was a small child again, snugly tucked up in bed, hearing her papa say, 'Goodnight, Corrie, I love you', and feeling the gentle touch of his hand.

She was a young woman sobbing her heart out, and her father was saying, 'God will give you a new kind of love for Karel, if you ask him to, Corrie'.

She was a resistance leader trying to help Jews, and a well-meaning friend was warning her father that he was too old and frail to risk being put in prison, but his reply had been firm: 'It would be an honour to give my life for God's ancient people, the Jews'.

She was standing in the Gestapo building in The Hague on their way to Scheveningen and a German officer was saying to her father, 'Old man, if you promise to behave yourself, I will let you go home and die in peace'.

His answer had ended all chance of a peaceful death: 'I shall continue to open my door to anyone in need.'

Corrie's tears fell again, but some of the sting had gone. 'Oh, Father, you wanted it this way,' she thought. 'And now you are in the presence of Jesus, and the wife you loved so much.' Then she prayed, 'Thank you, Lord, for comforting me. Please go on helping me and letting me feel you near me.'

***

The sky through the cell window was now the blue of early summer. Corrie drank in its brightness and dreamed of white sails, blue water and warm gold sand.

The cell door opened. It was Lieutenant Rahms again. 'You must come for the reading of your father's will,' he said. She followed him along a corridor and out into the sunshine. They walked into the hut.

Suddenly she was being hugged and kissed in turn by Willem, Betsie and Nollie, and then Tine and Flip. Willem looked strained and Betsie pale, but how good it was to see them, feel them, hear them.

The lieutenant stood at the far end of the room with his back to them, while they talked quietly together.

Corrie recognised, standing in the background, a lawyer from Haarlem, and smiled at him.

In low, hurried voices, family news and war news was passed on, producing a mixture of strong feelings.

Nollie handed Corrie a bag. She put a hand inside and pulled out – a tiny, whole Bible.

'I gave away my last gospel in the shower rooms only yesterday,' she whispered, beaming. Then she pushed the Bible and bag under her clothes.

All too soon the lieutenant turned round and said briskly, 'It's time to read the will.'

The lawyer came forward and read the short document.

'The house and shop are for Corrie and Betsie, as long as they need it. If it should be sold, remember my equal love for each of you. I commit you to God's care with great joy.'

'Let's pray,' said Willem. Corrie bowed her head and her brother said, 'Lord, watch over us and bless this good man who has given us this time together.'

Then it was time to part again.

Corrie was alone in her cell, reliving the past moments – the agony of learning that Father had died in a hospital corridor, sick, confused and alone, and had been buried in an unnamed grave ... the pain of knowing that Willem's blonde, handsome son, Kik, had been arrested while helping an American airman ... the sadness of hearing that Mary had unexpectedly walked out into the street and been arrested, and of imagining the growing fear and hunger in Haarlem as more men, more food, more goods were sent to Germany and life became even harder for the Jews, now 'disappearing' daily in large numbers.

But it was wonderful that they had been able to meet and talk, and good to know that the Russians were still pressing victoriously ahead in the east, and Britain and America in the south.

'All that, and a whole Bible too.' gloated Corrie.

She pulled a scarlet thread out of the towel which Nollie had sent her, and started embroidering another flower on her pyjama jacket. Since that parcel had arrived, she had added embroidery to her other activities of cell-pacing and letter-writing, ant-taming and sky-watching, praying and reading the Bible.

As she sewed, she prayed – for her family, her friends, the other prisoners, the lieutenant, and all those secretly or openly fighting the evil of Nazism.

'Lord,' she said, 'inside and outside prison, life is hard. Evil seems to be winning. But you are victor. Even here, in this lonely cell, I feel your presence and see your love. Bring this war and suffering and evil to an end, soon.'

She held up her pyjama jacket and inspected her work so far. Not bad. By the time she'd finished, the once-drab garment would be covered in bright, if not exactly artistic, shapes.

CAPTIVE IN VUGHT

'Betsie. Betsie. Over here.' Corrie shouted, trying to push her way through the seething mass of prisoners on the railway platform. After being alone for three months in Scheveningen, she felt bewildered by so many people.

They had been brought from the prison in vans and buses to this station outside The Hague. And it was here that she had spotted Betsie's chestnut head. Now her sister was doing her best to reach her.

They were face to face at last. In the middle of the crowds, they stood with arms round one another, laughing and crying. Then, hand-in-hand, they boarded the train, found a small space in a compartment and squeezed into it, and the journey began. There was so much to talk about – news of their family, their experiences in Scheveningen, their cell mates, the lieutenant ...

'He questioned me several times, Betsie,' said Corrie, 'and one day he picked up my file and threw all the papers on the fire.'

'He was a good man,' said Betsie. 'I went to him five times and each time he asked me to pray.'

'Let's pray we won't be separated again,' Corrie said, and her sister nodded.

'You help me so much,' she said. Then she asked, 'Where do you think we are going?'

'I don't know,' Corrie answered. 'But I pray it's not Germany.'

The train tunnelled through the darkness. The prisoners nearest the windows kept looking out, trying to see where they were. At last, one of them exclaimed, 'We're heading south.' Relief showed on all faces.

'Then it's not Germany,' thought Corrie. 'Thank you, Lord.'

The train stopped and the prisoners were ordered to get out. Bright searchlights were switched on to reveal that they were in a wood.

'Form ranks.' the guards shouted. In a few moments the prisoners were stumbling through the darkness, clutching the pillowcases which held their few possessions.

'Hurry, hurry.' the guards urged, prodding their backs with rifle butts. Betsie was pale and panting. Corrie took her pillowcase from her and put an arm round her.

In the grey pre-dawn light, they came to a barbed-wire fence, beyond which were wooden barracks.

Through the gates they marched and into one of these buildings. It was full of tables and benches. The prisoners collapsed on to the hard, wooden forms. When they had recovered a little, they gathered in groups to discuss where they were. Two women whom Betsie and Corrie knew from Haarlem, and had seen in the shower-rooms at Scheveningen, came across to join them.

'The village we passed was Vught,' said one of them, Mrs Bosman, 'so this must be Vught Concentration Camp.'

Concentration Camp. The words sent a shiver down Corrie's spine as she remembered terrible stories. 'Had they been the truth, or false rumours?' she wondered.

'But this isn't the main camp,' said the other woman, Leny Franse. 'Someone said they call it the quarantine compound, where newcomers stay for a few weeks.'

Corrie and Betsie were trying to write letters but it wasn't easy. At the far end of the barracks a fight was in progress. It had started as a quarrel but then tempers had been lost and other prisoners had joined in, so that now the shouting and screaming were terrible.

A guard was intervening. The sound of her slaps, kicks and curses only added to the general hubbub.

'What a way to run a camp.' thought Corrie. 'Hundreds of women crowded together all day with nothing to do. No wonder there is so much quarrelling. Our guards haven't any idea of how to handle us.'

She thought back to camps she had run for their girls' club, remembering the activities and the fun ...

'Oh, Corrie, things are getting very bad in this place,' said Betsie, beside her. 'We must start a club. The rules will be: one, no grumbling, and two, join others to pray for the barracks.'

Within a fortnight Betsie's prayer group was making a difference to the atmosphere.

The sisters were standing in line waiting to report for rope making. The officer in charge of the women guards came to them. She was known as 'the general' – and was hated and feared for her cold cruelty.

'Prisoners ten Boom Elizabeth and ten Boom Cornelia. Report to the administration barracks at nine o'clock in the morning,' she said, handing them some pink forms. Then she was gone.

Friends gathered round to look at the papers. One said, 'You're going to be set free. We're so happy for you.'

The sisters stared at each other, a wild hope shining in their eyes. Then they looked at the sad faces of their friends.

'The war will soon be over, and you'll all be free,' said Betsie. 'Then you must come and stay with us in Haarlem. We would love to have you.'

'That's right,' added Corrie. 'It can't be long before the Allies recapture France and liberate the rest of Europe.'

The sisters shared out their things among the others.

They wouldn't be needing them now.

***

They stood, the next morning, outside the administration barracks in the sunshine. There was a sudden flapping of wings from the top of a silver birch tree, and a heron winged its way across the countryside beyond the electrified barbed wire. Soon they, too, would be free. When their turn came, they moved to the desk and were handed their money, watches and rings.

'This is it.' thought Corrie excitedly. 'Any moment now we'll be walking out of this place ...'

They were taken to a barracks near the gates. There was another long wait, but with such high hopes, they didn't mind. Corrie was dreaming of seeing Willem and Nollie and her nephews and nieces again. Then she noticed Betsie's change of expression and turned to see what had upset her.

Two prisoners were being made to run from one barracks to the next. They were nearly dropping from exhaustion, but the German officer, cycling along behind them, was smiling, enjoying their suffering.

Corrie put an arm round her sister, and closed her eyes to pray. The man standing next to them said quietly, 'That's right – pray. We shall certainly need all the prayer we can get.'

'We do pray,' Betsie answered. 'But aren't we going to be set free?'

'Oh, no.' the man replied, his face showing sympathy for their dashed hopes. 'It'll be the bunkers for us, or worse, I'm afraid.'

The bunkers. The sisters looked at each other with shocked expressions – remembering a man they had seen coming out of one of these small, dark punishment cells. He had been a pitiful sight – more dead than alive. More waiting followed, and then a walk to another office, where their money, watches and rings were taken away again. Then another walk, another wait, another officer sitting at a desk. They presented their forms to him, and stood there, with fast-beating hearts.

'Transferred to main camp,' he said.

'No freedom, but at least no bunkers,' was Corrie's first thought.

Corrie was once again sitting at a work bench, but it was nothing like the one she had in her father's shop. She looked round at the huge barracks where she and hundreds of women sat day after day, helping to make radios for the Germans.

It was certainly a change from Scheveningen. The factory was some distance from the main camp at Vught, and they worked there for eleven hours every day, except Sundays when they were free from lunch-time onwards.

'Well, Miss ten Boom,' said a voice behind Corrie, 'you are the first prisoner I have had who seems interested in her work.' Corrie turned to smile at the speaker. She had watched him walking round the barracks and noticed his kind manner. He was a fellow-prisoner but the Germans had put him in charge of the work in this part of the factory.

'I am a watchmaker, Mr Moorman,' she told him.

'A watchmaker. Then I must find some more interesting work for you. Come.' He led her to another part of the room and motioned her to a seat.

'I myself was a headmaster before the war,' he said. Corrie knew that the camp was full of people like him – decent, kind, well-educated, skilled men and women who had been snatched from homes and work and loved ones ...

The man began to explain Corrie's new job to her.

'It's only checking switches – not nearly as interesting as watchmaking, I'm afraid, but I hope not as dull as measuring glass rods.' he said. Corrie watched and listened.

'I think I know what to do now,' she said. 'Thank you, Mr Moorman.'

'Just call if you need me,' he said, with a smile, and walked away.

Corrie mastered the work quickly and soon her thoughts were free to fly about. She remembered the walk to the factory that morning – the beauty of the sunrise reddening the eastern sky and turning each dewdrop into a diamond, the liquid notes of a lark, the fresh tangy smells, the varying shades of green. 'If it weren't for the roll calls, life wouldn't be too bad, considering,' she thought. But those hours of standing to attention before and after work were just too much. Roll call that morning had lasted two hours, and then a guard had announced that some of the beds hadn't been made neatly enough, so there'd be no letters or parcels for any of them for a month ...

A sudden burst of conversation told her that the guards had left the room. She glanced round and saw women prisoners bringing out food, knitting and games, or going over to talk to their friends. Corrie had already made friends with some of her fellow-workers, and two came across to her workbench.

'Congratulations on your promotion.' said one. 'How are you getting on?'

'Fine, thanks,' said Corrie. The other woman shook her head at Corrie's finished work, and said, 'Looks as though you are getting on too well, as usual. We're working for the Germans, remember, and the motto is, "Go slow and slip in as many mistakes as possible."'

'I'm sorry,' answered Corrie, 'I do try to remember, but it goes against the grain to do shoddy work.'

As the prisoners talked, planes roared across the brilliant, blue sky above them. British and American planes – they all hoped. 'Thick clouds.' came the warning from the look-outs. Corrie's friends went hurriedly back to their places. By the time the guards stepped into the building, not a thing or person was out of place.

For lunch there was watery porridge. Corrie washed her hands first, taking care not to talk to the 'cleaning man'. Last time she'd done so, a guard had reported her, and she'd been given a stern warning. Next time, it might be much worse. Then she joined her friends outside to eat and chat. She began to feel very sleepy.

'I think I'll have a nap,' she said, and went indoors to lie on a bench.

She had been up since half-past four that morning, and there was a long, hot afternoon of work ahead, followed by roll call and the march back. But at least she had Betsie to look forward to. She pictured her sister, sitting in the dormitory, sewing prison uniforms with the other less-fit prisoners.

The day's work ended at last, and the factory-party marched back to the main camp. Before they reached the women's area, they passed the men's compound. Male prisoners had shaved heads and wore striped prison suits. Some were standing as close to the fence as they dared, hoping to exchange whispered messages or glances with the women.

'My husband's in there,' the girl next to Corrie whispered. 'I haven't seen him for days – I hope he's all right.' Corrie grieved for her, and others separated from husbands, sons, sweethearts.

'There he is.' the woman exclaimed softly, and raised a hand to wave. The next minute she dropped it to her side, as the harsh voice of a guard shouted, 'No communication with the male prisoners.' She added threateningly, 'Do that again and you'll go to the bunkers.'

'Oh, Lord,' prayed Corrie. 'We are no longer shut up in prison cells, but I see now that the same evil that was in Scheveningen is in Vught. Thank you that Betsie and I are together, and help us to bring your light to the people around us.'

They were now entering the women's camp, and there was Betsie, waiting at the door of the dormitory, a smile of welcome on her face. Corrie ran to hug her. Then they sat down to share each other's news.

'I'm on a new workbench,' said Corrie. 'It's better there and our supervisor is such a kind man.'

'I'm so glad.' said Betsie. After a short pause, she added, 'We had a new lady in our sewing group today.'

'Who was she? Do we know her? Did she have any news?' asked Corrie, eagerly, but Betsie looked suddenly very sad.

'Remember that man who came and asked you for money the day we were arrested?' she said.

'Of course I remember him. I dragged myself out of bed to go and see him.'

'Well, this woman knows all about him. His name is Jan Vogel and he's been working for the Nazis ever since the occupation. It was through him that we, and many others, were betrayed.'

Corrie sat still, digesting this information. Jan Vogel. The man responsible for all that had happened to them – and to Father. She saw, in her mind, his dear, suffering face, and felt a sudden, strong upsurge of anger towards the man who had caused it.

'I'll never forgive him for what he did to Father,' she vowed, silently, 'never.' Betsie was looking at her with brown eyes full of sympathy, but Corrie turned away.

A few friends began to gather round the sisters for their usual time of prayer and Bible reading. Betsie fished their Bible out of the pouch which hung under her clothes, and offered it to her sister.

'No, you lead this evening,' said Corrie.

***

It was going to be another long night. Corrie lay on her bunk staring into the darkness. The past few days and nights had crawled by. The strain was becoming unbearable.

'Betsie.'

'Yes, Corrie.'

'Don't you feel anything towards that man – that Jan Vogel?'

'Of course I do. I never stop praying for him. He must be suffering terribly.'

Corrie was speechless. She shut her eyes and felt tears trickling down her cheeks as she prayed, 'I give in, Lord. Betsie's right and I'm wrong. Please forgive me and take away my hatred for this man, Jan Vogel. I ask you to bless him and his family.'

The strain had gone. Peacefully, she drifted into sleep.
***

Sunny days, weeks and months passed.

'We're half-way through August,' said Corrie. 'So by September we shall have been prisoners for six months – and I've heard that's the usual term for ration card offenders, like us.'

'But Corrie, we don't know for sure,' warned Betsie.

They were sitting outside on a log bench one Sunday evening. The air was warm and filled with birdsong. The sandy ground under their feet shone like satin and was broken up by shrubs and flowers. Beyond the walls lay a meadow, a cluster of farm buildings, and a small wood.

'In any case,' persisted Corrie, 'the war must end soon. The British and American troops are winning victories all the time. It can't be long before they push the Germans right out of France.'

'In the meantime, there is so much work for us to do here,' said Betsie.

'I know,' said Corrie, thinking of the service she had led that afternoon and the talks she and Betsie had had with different women afterwards. 'People are so eager to hear more about God's love and power.'

As she spoke, she was watching some of the other prisoners talking and moving about, in their blue overalls with the red stripes down them. Most of them looked brown and fit. It was especially good to see healthy children after the pale washed-out waifs of Scheveningen.

She picked out some of the people she knew – such a large number now. There was Mrs Boileau, whose sons had been shot. How bright she always was. And Lily from Switzerland, and plump, jolly Janneke from Belgium, and Marie, whose husband had been murdered before her eyes, and Mrs Diederiks, whose husband had just been shot and who was carrying her first baby, and Mrs Bosman who had tried to escape, and been punished by having to sit all night on the floor of the soldiers' dormitory. None of them should be in a place like this. There shouldn't be places like Vught.

Something was happening. A group of prisoners had come from somewhere else in the camp and were moving about talking to people. Wherever they went, faces became animated.

'There must be some news,' Corrie thought. 'Good news.'

She glanced at her sister, but Betsie looked as though she had fallen asleep. She was about to get up and find out what was happening, when Marie came running across. She crouched down beside them, and said, 'The Dutch forces are approaching Belgium.'

'That's wonderful.' exclaimed Corrie, but Betsie opened her eyes, and asked quietly, 'Is it true?'

'Yes, most people seem to be pretty sure about it,' Marie answered. The next moment she was cowering, her hands over her ears, as the peace of the evening was torn apart by a shattering explosion of sound. Several more ear-splitting bangs followed. When nothing had been heard for a while, the prisoners uncovered their ears.

'Betsie, are you all right?' asked Corrie.

'I think so,' said Betsie. 'What do you think it was?'

'I'll see if I can find out,' said Marie, jumping up to join one of the groups busily discussing what had happened. In a few moments she came back, her pretty eyes bright.

'They think the Germans are blowing up bridges to slow down the Dutch forces.' she announced.

'Then they must be near, very near.' exclaimed Corrie.

For days rumours flew about the camp, and the prisoners waited, torn between hope and fear ...

'Come quickly. There's something going on in the men's camp.' At the urgency in Leny's voice, Betsie and Corrie hurried after her to the fence. In their compound, the men were standing to attention. The women were too far away to recognise individuals or hear what numbers the guards were calling out, but they could see that a group of men were being singled out – for something.

'What is going to happen? My husband is there – somewhere.' said one woman, her eyes wide with terror. Corrie couldn't answer. There were now about two hundred men in the separate group. The guards stopped calling out numbers, and gave a command. The group marched out through the gate. The sound of their footsteps dwindled and then died. The tension among the women was at its peak. One ran into the barracks and others followed, unable to bear it.

A shot shattered the silence, and then another and another and another ... one hundred and eighty shots. One hundred and eighty decent, kind Hollanders – fathers, sons, sweethearts, husbands – dead in the dust.

Corrie was utterly crushed. 'Oh, Betsie, I can't bear this,' she whispered. All around them were women who had no idea whether their loved ones were now among the living or the dead.

She looked into her sister's face. It was serene.

'Almost as though the evil hasn't been allowed to touch her,' thought Corrie. She took her hand and led her to the back of the barracks. There, on a little log bench, they sat side-by-side in silence. What Betsie was thinking, Corrie didn't know, but her own heart was crying out in silent agony, 'Why, Lord? This is too much. I can't bear it.'

Suddenly, the years rolled back and she saw herself as a child, talking to her father. They were on a train travelling home after papa's weekly trip to check the time by the big clock in Amsterdam. She had been telling him about a word she had heard.

'What does it mean?' she'd asked, looking eagerly into the kind, bearded face. He had pointed to his large suitcase and answered, 'Would you carry that for me please, Corrie?'

How she'd struggled with that case, wanting to please papa. 'I can't manage it,' she'd admitted sadly.

Now, more than forty years later, his reply came back to her. 'Of course you can't, Corrie. And I would be a bad father to expect you to carry such a heavy case. It is the same with your question. The answer would be too heavy for you to bear, so please let me bear it for you, until you are old enough to take it on yourself.'

Back in the present, Corrie prayed, 'I cannot bear this thing that has happened. Please bear it for me, and help me to trust you.'

The heartache eased a little and the pain became less sharp.

'Come, Betsie, let's go back to those poor women,' she said. 'They will be badly in need of God's comfort.'

⏱ TO GERMANY WITH DREAD ⏱

Corrie felt sick. She and Betsie, with all the other prisoners, had been standing to attention for hours, while guards cleared out Vught Concentration Camp. Piles of rubbish kept being thrown into the ovens to burn. Smoke filled the air with acrid fumes.

'September has come and we have not been released,' Corrie thought, numbly. And the future held possibilities too terrible for words.

Long cars were passing. She peered through a window in one of these, and caught sight of pale, wasted faces. 'The sick from the hospital,' she thought.

At last the order came – 'March.'

Corrie put an arm round Betsie and they walked as quickly as they could, out past the gates of Vught. They had been there nearly three months. Now, as they marched away, the countryside was breathtakingly beautiful, but there was dread in every heart.

They neared some railway tracks. Ahead, Corrie could see shaved heads and striped suits by the thousand, as the male prisoners waited at a siding. An order came and they climbed aboard the wooden carriages.

'A goods train – as though we were luggage or coal,' thought Corrie. Beside her, Betsie was now very white and breathless.

'Nearly there,' Corrie told her. Clinging to each other, they reached the lines and climbed into one of the trucks. They found a space near one of the walls and sat there, hunched up, as more people kept piling in.

'There must be nearly eighty in here now,' Corrie said. She felt hot and sticky and the smell of bodies turned her stomach.

'Air – I must have air.' a faint voice called. A tough-looking woman opposite started prizing a nail out of the wall near her. When it came free, she used it to try and widen the hole it had left. Others began doing the same. It was good to feel more air coming in.

'Oh, Betsie,' said Corrie, in dismay, 'people are sitting on our bread supply.' Loaves had been piled in a corner and now women were using them as seats.

'I suppose they have nowhere else to sit,' said Betsie. There was a jolt and the journey began.

Betsie could peer out through a crack near her, and in between dozing she would describe what she saw.

'There's a little wood. I can almost smell the pines, Corrie. We're passing a canal now. I can see a boat. A boy is waving at the train. I wish I could wave back ...'

Suddenly they heard a series of sharp bangs and the train jerked to a stop.

'Shooting,' someone said, and everyone cowered and waited.

'We're near the border,' someone else said. 'It must be the resistance, trying to rescue us.' The words produced ripples of excitement and hope.

'Let them succeed.' thought Corrie, her arms round Betsie.

The shooting continued for a few moments, then stopped, and the train rolled on. Hope died on everyone's faces, eyes stared dully ahead again.

'We are now in Germany,' someone said. The words sounded like a curse.

'Oh, Lord,' prayed Corrie, her heart very heavy, 'I have asked so often that you would not send us to Germany, but here we are. Lord, we are weak and sick and we cry to you for help.'

Betsie was peeking out again.

'The fields are so beautiful with the sun shining on them, and in the distance are hills with silver streams running down them.'

Corrie remembered a holiday in Germany with her club girls. The sun had been shining then, too, as they had hiked their way along the River Rhine ...

'Now we are coming into a town,' Betsie continued. 'Oh, Corrie, how different things are here. Huge holes and mounds of rubble everywhere.'

Days and nights merged as they dozed, talked or simply sat. There was plenty of bread for everyone but the stench in the compartment meant Corrie felt too sick to eat. Soon thirst was her greatest problem.

Now and again, pails of water were brought to the door, but the women nearest to it snatched greedily at them and drank their fill. By the time a pail reached Corrie and Betsie, it was usually empty or nearly so.

At Oranienburg, the train stopped and the men's coaches were uncoupled, but the women's were pulled on, deeper and deeper into Germany.

Corrie's whole body was now craving for a drink. She began to feel feverish and light-headed. At last, some water was brought to her. Betsie held a mug to her lips and she drank and drank, and afterwards fell into a troubled sleep.

The train stopped.

'Out. Out. Everyone out.' came the welcome order. Thousands of women struggled wearily out of the carriages to stand about, gulping in fresh air and stretching cramped limbs.

Betsie and Corrie propped each other up, enjoying the sun on their skin, the wind in their hair and the clean, fresh smells.

'Poor Corrie, you're sick,' said Betsie.

'I feel better already,' Corrie answered. 'Where are we?'

'I heard someone say Furstenberg,' said Betsie.

After a while, the guards ordered the women to form ranks of five and march. Corrie's legs felt very weak. Betsie and the woman on her other side supported her on the long journey. On and on they trudged – an endless line of prisoners, clutching blankets and pillowcases. Only a few guards were needed to supervise such weak and exhausted women.

They were allowed to stop and rest once. Corrie collapsed on the grass beside a lake and thought of 'green pastures and still waters'. Around them rose hills and trees, and not far away was a white-spired church.

'Yea, though I walk through the valley of the shadow of death, I will fear no evil ...' she thought.

It was time to move on. Putting one foot in front of another became almost mechanical after a while.

And then they saw it, lying below them, like a hideous bruise on the beautiful face of the countryside.

'Ravensbruck,' whispered the woman beside Corrie. The sisters gripped each other's hands and stared down at the vast city of grey barracks, with its tall watch-towers and, most chilling of all, its huge central smoking chimney stack.

Down they marched, nearer and nearer to the women's concentration camp about which so many ugly stories had been told. 'Are they true?' Corrie wondered. They would soon find out.

Now they could see the coils of barbed wire topping the tall, thick double concrete walls, and the signs, each bearing a skull and crossbones to warn prisoners of the electric current pulsing through the twisting steel.

The massive gates swung open to receive them. A woman started to sing and more and more voices took up her song.

'Oh yes, oh yes, you Netherlands women,

Heads up, heads up, heads up.'

Corrie felt proud of her fellow countrywomen, as she and Betsie joined in the singing.

At the same time, she was looking around, gathering her first impressions of the place.

On either side of the entrance stood the Ravensbruck guards. The men wore caps, decorated with skulls and crossbones, and blue uniforms. They carried machine guns. The women wore grey suits and swung snake-like whips. But it was their expressions which told Corrie most. Never, not even in Scheveningen, had she seen faces as depraved and evil as these. She felt certain that their minds were busily plotting ways of wiping the smiles off the faces of the bravely singing women.

She shuddered and turned away from this guard of honour to look at some of the other inmates of the camp. There were plenty of them about, all wearing the same sort of dresses, with 'X's sewn into the material back and front. The first group she saw going off to work somewhere looked fairly fit, but they were young, she noticed, and possibly healthy.

And then she saw others, and her spirits dropped to zero. They were walking skeletons, stretching out claw-like hands to the new prisoners and begging for food. The female guards beat them back.

Corrie and Betsie flinched and drew closer together. They reached a huge open-sided tent and were at last told to stop marching. They swarmed under the canvas, collapsing on to the straw which was covering the ground.

'Oh, Betsie, it's full of lice.' said Corrie, but they were too tired to move.

'It would be better to have short hair,' said Betsie, quietly. Corrie was horrified, but saw that her sister was right. She borrowed a pair of scissors from another prisoner, and cut the thick, chestnut locks while tears poured down her cheeks. It felt like the last straw.

'Get out. Move. Hurry.'

There was to be no peace. The women left the tent, formed ranks and stood to attention. Daylight faded. A chill wind sprang up and started to blow round them.

'They're going to leave us here all night,' someone said.

'Surely not,' thought Corrie. But soon all around her, women were spreading out blankets and settling down on them. The sisters made themselves as comfortable as possible and slept. In the middle of the night it rained, soaking them to their skins. Corrie shivered and worried about Betsie. In the morning, the weary prisoners wrung out their wet things and waited. Thin, brown liquid and a slice of black bread were given to each of them, then nothing more until the afternoon when turnip soup and boiled potatoes were dished out.

'What are they trying to do to us?' Corrie wondered. 'Betsie won't be able to stand much more of this.' Her own legs were aching from the long hours of standing at attention. But no orders were given, and for the second night the women settled down to sleep on the ground – wrapped in damp blankets.

Betsie and Corrie lay close together, looking up at the stars and praying till they fell asleep. During the night Betsie started having sharp pains in her stomach.

Corrie wrapped a sweater round her and gave her some vitamin drops. Another day dawned, and still the women were left standing stiffly to attention.

'Are they trying to break our spirits, to punish us for daring to enter Ravensbruck singing?' Corrie wondered.

At the end of the day there were some orders at last. 'Line up for the bath house.'

Corrie took Betsie's arm and helped her to where the shower-rooms were. They waited outside, moving slowly forward as more women entered the place.

Corrie looked at the prisoners emerging from the bath house and her heart sank. They were wearing thin prison undershirts and dresses and wooden shoes and were carrying only a few washing things in their hands.

'No warm clothes and no Bible, how will we bear it?' asked Corrie silently. She turned to her sister.

'Betsie, God is asking us to give up everything we own. Are you ready for this sacrifice?' she asked gently.

Betsie's normal serene face crumpled suddenly and she started to cry.

'No, Corrie, I'm not. I can't bear it,' she said brokenly.

Corrie put her arms round the thin, shaking shoulders and prayed, 'Lord, if you are asking this of us, give us your strength.' She felt her sister grow calm again, then heard her say quietly, 'I'm ready now.'

Their turn came at last. They went inside and stood under the harsh glare of naked light bulbs, looking at the pile of confiscated goods near the door – blankets, food, and pillowcases filled with clothes, books and other little treasures and comforts.

Corrie and Betsie added their blankets and pillowcases to the heap, but not before Corrie had fished out her little bottle of vitamin drops.

'I must have those – Betsie needs them,' she thought. When she came to the checking-in desk, she put the bottle down with her washing things. The woman looked at it, then pushed it into the bag with the other things, and moved her on.

'What a relief. Thank you, Lord,' thought Corrie. She waited for Betsie and together they moved towards the desk where women were having to strip and walk naked to the shower-rooms.

'I need the bathroom,' said Betsie faintly, clutching her stomach. Corrie spoke to the guard.

'Please may we use the toilets?' she asked. The woman pointed to a door. Corrie led Betsie towards it. They stepped inside and looked around. The toilets were holes in the floor. The place was empty except for a stack of decaying benches in a corner.

Suddenly Corrie had an idea. 'Quick, Betsie,' she whispered. 'Take off your woollen underwear and the blue sweater and then slip your overall back on.' Her sister did so. Corrie removed her underwear too, then she took the Bible in its bag from round her neck and wrapped it up in the clothes. It was the work of a few seconds to tuck the bundle behind the benches before rejoining the queue.

They stripped, had their showers and put on the prison clothes. While Betsie waited in the check-out line, Corrie returned to the room with the benches in it, snatched up the bundle and pushed it down under her dress. Flattening the things out as best she could, she prayed, 'Lord, please put your angels round me – only this time let them not be invisible.'

Back in line, she smiled confidently at Betsie when she whispered, 'I can see the bumps quite clearly, Corrie.'

'Don't worry,' she told her. 'The guards will not see them because they won't see me.'

They reached the first inspection point. Just ahead of them was a girl with a lump under her clothes. She was searched and a woollen vest was found and taken from her. It was Corrie's turn next. She walked past – and nothing happened. The guards didn't seem to notice her. Betsie, behind her was searched.

Corrie walked towards the second check-out point. Here the guards were running their hands over the prisoners, feeling for anything hidden under their clothes. Corrie went past them, unchallenged. It was as though they had not seen her ...

She stood outside, waiting for Betsie, with a feeling of hope.

'Lord, if you answer prayer like this, then I can face even Ravensbruck,' she said. Betsie came out, saw the light in her sister's face, and smiled her warm, bright smile.

They were taken to Barracks 8 – the quarantine barracks for newcomers. In it were two large rooms and two smaller ones, with bunks three tiers high on every wall.

Corrie and Betsie were sitting on their bit of mattress, talking. They had been in the quarantine barracks for several days now and were exhausted from the roll calls.

'They're just trying to wear us out, I'm sure of it,' said Corrie. 'Yesterday was almost one long roll call, starting at half past four and ending late at night. I was so worried about you.'

'I'm all right,' said Betsie. 'And I'm sure God has put us here for a reason. So many women are joining us now for our times of prayer and Bible reading. I can see their faces lighting up as they listen.'

Harsh voices were shouting orders. 'Not another roll call,' said Corrie.

'It sounds like medical inspection,' said Betsie. They joined the others going out of the barracks, and listened. This time they heard the order clearly.

'Report at hospital barracks for medical inspection.'

The prisoners walked over to the building. Corrie and Betsie had to wait for a long time outside. At last they stepped into the corridor.

'Take off your clothes and leave them at the entrance,' barked a guard.

'Oh, no. Not a naked parade in front of these men.' thought Corrie. She gave Betsie a sympathetic look, knowing exactly how she was feeling. Together, they stood naked and shivering with cold and shame. They gripped each other's hands, to gain strength to bear the sneering looks and coarse remarks of their guards. The doctors they were supposed to be seeing were not even sitting at the desk.

Suddenly Corrie remembered a painting she had once seen of Jesus on the cross. It struck her for the first time, recalling that picture, that he had endured nakedness, too.

'How that must have added to his other sufferings,' she thought.

'Lord, I never realised before that you hung naked on the cross for us. Now I understand a little of what it must have cost you to suffer in that way. Thank you for bearing that for me. Help me to bear this for you.'

Her body continued to shrink and shiver, but inside her was a feeling of warm joy.

Three medical people arrived – two doctors and a dentist.

The prisoners started filing past them. One looked them briefly up and down, another peered into their mouths, and the third inspected their fingers.

'So the stripping wasn't really necessary,' thought Corrie. 'Just another way of humiliating us, I suppose.'

***

Corrie was using her half-hour of freedom before bedtime to take a walk, but it wasn't proving a pleasant one. She had already passed the detention barracks which housed women under the death sentence and those waiting to be used as human guinea pigs, and the guardhouse, which was kept for the 'worst offenders' – one of whom was even then being flogged.

And now another prisoner had drawn her attention to a tiny concrete cell. In it, leaning against the wall, was a retarded child, with nothing on except a short vest.

'Do you know,' the prisoner said, 'that child has been in there for weeks, on half-rations, and sleeping on the concrete floor with no blanket. It's amazing that she's alive, let alone able to stand.'

Corrie's heart ached for the girl, and she longed to take the thin body in her arms. She turned away from the window with tears in her eyes, praying, 'Lord, please take this little one into your loving arms soon. And please let me be released soon so that I can open a home for children like her.'

She went to find Betsie, thinking, 'Even if we're not set free, I hope at least we'll be moved from the quarantine barracks. Things will be better in the main camp. At least, they can't be much worse.'

⏱ PRISONER 66730 IN ⏱ RAVENSBRUCK

'Oh, Betsie, what have we come to?' asked Corrie, in despairing tones. They were standing where the guards had left them, in the middle of a vast dormitory inside Barracks 28 – their new permanent quarters, after several weeks in the quarantine block.

The room was gloomy and stank. A few windows had glass in, but the rest were stuffed with rags or newspapers. Everywhere they looked there were square platforms, three tiers high. In between, were very narrow aisles.

'It will not be easy,' Betsie admitted, slowly, 'but the Lord will show us how to cope.'

'He will have to,' thought Corrie, as all her hopes that things would be better, died. She could hear other new arrivals clambering on to their straw mattresses.

Suddenly there was a crash and a shout. A woman had fallen through the slats of her platform, and crashed on to the tier below, bringing loose straws, dust and dirt with her. 'Probably happens all the time,' thought Corrie, noticing some of the wide gaps between the slats on nearby platforms.

They helped the woman clear up the mess and then returned to their own. The guard had pointed out where they were to sleep – on the second tier. 'You and seven others there,' she had said, pointing to a space big enough for about four people.

'Well, we'd better practise getting up,' said Corrie. Betsie hauled herself up with her sister helping from below and then following her. They lay on the straw mattress, staring up at the slats above. Corrie tried to sit up, but there was not enough space.

'The blankets are very dirty,' she commented. The next moment she was climbing hastily down exclaiming, 'Fleas, Betsie. The mattress is crawling with them.' But Betsie seemed to be miles away.

'Oh, look, they're on the bottom mattress, too,' said Corrie. 'This is horrible.'

'Corrie,' said Betsie, sounding strangely excited.

'Yes.'

'God has shown me how we can bear all this. He has said that we must give thanks in all circumstances, so let's start now.'

'Give thanks for this?' queried Corrie, astonished.

'Well, we can thank him that we're still together, and that we have our Bible and the warm underwear and vitamin drops.'

'That's true,' Corrie answered, and bowed her head to praise God for these blessings.

'We thank you for the people,' prayed Betsie but before Corrie could put in her 'Amen' she continued, 'We also praise you for the fleas.'

'Now that is taking things a bit too far,' thought Corrie, giving Betsie a fondly disapproving look.

People were now coming into the barracks. They were women returning from their places of work.

'Looks as though we're about to meet our seven bedfellows,' Corrie said, adding, 'I wonder what work we will be given.'

***

'How much longer will we be able to stand this back-breaking work?' Corrie wondered, as she and Betsie pushed a heavy cart along.

'Faster. Faster.' screamed a guard, and lashed out with her whip. It stung Corrie's neck, but the pain was nothing compared with what she felt as she heard Betsie gasping for breath beside her.

The factory where they had been working for several weeks now was a mile and a half from the camp. The early morning march took them past houses and streets with ordinary, free people in them, but Corrie hadn't even managed to exchange friendly glances with them. They all averted their eyes as the prisoners approached.

Corrie longed to feast her eyes on the late autumn countryside. But there was no time. Besides, the wind was chilly as it sought out the holes in their tattered clothes, and standing around wasn't a good idea.

They had reached the railway tracks, and it was time to stop and haul heavy metal plates out of the goods vans standing there, load up their cart with them and push it back to the factory gates.

Corrie fished out from under her clothes some packing material she had managed to find. She wrapped this round Betsie's hands to protect them a little against the biting cold of the iron they would be handling.

Working in silence, they filled their cart and then started pushing it back along the way they had come – only now it was much, much heavier. Corrie glanced up at the sky and was reassured by the position of the sun.

'Not long now, Betsie,' she whispered encouragingly. Her sister was too breathless to reply, but she gave Corrie a bright, sweet smile.

Corrie was feeling famished. Early that morning they had had a few mouthfuls of so-called coffee and a slice of black bread. Then at midday there had been a mug of warm soup – thin with a few lumps of potato in it. That had been all. But her greatest longing just then was not for food. What her aching legs and blistered hands craved for was rest ...

At last they were given the order to form ranks and march back. Betsie was almost collapsing by the time they reached the camp, but there was no rest yet. They stood in long food queues for their ration of soup, which was so quickly eaten.

Free at last. Corrie supported Betsie as they went into their dormitory and collapsed on to a bunk.

'Amazing what a difference a short rest can make,' thought Corrie. She went and fished out her bottle of vitamins, and took them to Betsie.

'I suppose you've been handing this round to everyone else, as usual,' she commented.

'Oh, only to a few,' her sister answered, then opened her mouth to receive three drops from the tilted bottle.

'There really can't be more than a few drops left now,' said Corrie, screwing the lid on, and putting the bottle back.

'You've been saying that for weeks,' Betsie pointed out, laughing.

'I know I have,' agreed Corrie. 'I can't understand why the bottle wasn't empty long ago.'

'Don't try to understand it,' said Betsie. 'Just accept it as one of God's many miracles of love to us. Now then, what about our service?'

'Are you sure you are well enough?'

'Yes, I'm all right. Will you lead? And I'll pray afterwards.'

The sisters spoke to some of the women nearby and then went to the back of the room where there was just enough light to read by. Corrie drew the Bible out of its bag under her clothes and started turning the pages and praying that God would give her a message, while women from all over the barracks were gathering to listen. These were old friends from Vught, new friends made since coming to Ravensbruck, and others whom they hardly knew at all.

Corrie looked round at them – women from different countries and backgrounds, but all passing through times of suffering and hardship ... young ones, like pretty Marie, middle-aged ones like Betsie and herself, and very old ones, like Mrs Leness.

Then she looked down at her open Bible and read, 'For I am persuaded that neither death, nor life, nor angels, nor principalities, nor powers, nor things present, nor things to come, nor height, nor depth, nor any other creature, shall be able to separate us from the love of God which is in Christ Jesus our Lord'.

She paused, looked up and went on, 'We are not separated from his love even here. Nothing they can do to us in Ravensbruck can separate us from his love. If we belong to Jesus, we experience this truth for ourselves.' The women listened eagerly as she spoke. Those who were bilingual quietly translated the words into other languages for those who couldn't understand Dutch.

Afterwards, Betsie prayed.

***

Roll call time again.

'I think we shall have to think about having another service after evening roll calls,' said Betsie, as she and Corrie walked towards the space where the women from Barracks 28 had to line up. 'More and more people are wanting to come and join us.'

'Yes, I feel that God is speaking to many people in the darkness of this place,' answered Corrie. 'It's amazing that we are left in peace most of the time. In the centre room there are always guards patrolling round, but very few seem to bother with our large dormitory.'

The tedium of roll call began. She hoped there would be no hitches tonight, as she wanted to get Betsie to bed, and she was feeling weary too. Back in the dormitory, Mien greeted them, clutching a bag. She was a friend from Haarlem who now worked at the hospital.

'Vitamin pills.' she announced, speaking quietly. 'I managed to take a little from each jar, so that no one would notice.'

'Thank you, Mien.' said Betsie, and Corrie exclaimed, 'This is wonderful. Now I can give Betsie the last few vitamin drops.' She drew out the bottle, unscrewed the lid, and turned it over just above Betsie's open mouth. Nothing happened. She shook it. Not a drop came out.

Betsie closed her mouth, then said simply, 'The miracle was no longer needed.'

***

At last, work at the factory finished. Corrie and Betsie were assigned to a weapons factory, and told to report for medical inspection.

They stood outside the medical barracks with the other prisoners. Corrie asked one of these, 'Can you tell us what work at the weapons factory is like?'

'I'm told that working conditions and food are better there than here,' the woman replied. 'Just the thought of living away from this place makes me feel good.'

Corrie and Betsie looked hopefully at one another.

When their numbers were called out, they went into the building, stripped and paraded naked in front of the doctor. He looked scornfully at Betsie's thin body and white face and said, 'Rejected.'

It was Corrie's turn next. 'Approved,' said the doctor.

The sisters exchanged horrified glances. Now Betsie would be found working inside the camp, while Corrie lived and worked at the weapons factory.

'Lord, please don't let me be separated from Betsie,' Corrie prayed desperately. 'She needs me.'

She had now moved on to a desk where a woman sat testing the prisoners' eyesight.

'Read the letters.' said the woman, pointing to her chart. Corrie stumbled over them, pretending that she couldn't see them properly.

The woman gave her a sharp look, and asked, 'Don't you want to work at the weapons factory?'

'Oh, no.' said Corrie eagerly. 'You see, my sister is sick and needs me.'

'Come and see me about new glasses tomorrow,' said the woman, handing Corrie a slip of paper. She looked at it anxiously – and then smiled. What a relief. It said she was to report at half past six – just when the work crew would be leaving for the weapons factory.

Next morning, as the lorries drove out of the gates, Corrie reported to the medical building. An official looked at her and said, 'You're not allowed in without one of your guards.' Corrie turned away and walked round until she saw the guard whom the prisoners called 'The Snake'.

'Prisoner 66730 ten Boom Cornelia reporting,' she said, going up to the woman. 'Please would you take me to see about new glasses?' The Snake waved her hand, saying, 'I'm too busy – find the other guard.' Corrie went in search of this woman, and at last found her, only to be told, 'I haven't got time to go with you.'

Corrie wondered what she was to do next? She went to tell Betsie what had happened. A guard spotted them standing idle and shouted, 'Report for knitting duty.'

The sisters were delighted. They hurried towards Barracks 28. The centre of the room was full of women knitting grey woolly army socks. The supervisor wrote their numbers in a black book and said, pointing, 'There's the wool and the instructions. But you'll have to work in the dormitory. There's no more room here.'

Corrie and Betsie picked up their materials and went into their dormitory feeling almost light-hearted.

'We'll be together, indoors and out of the cold, and doing light work.' thought Corrie, gratefully.

Clickety-clack went the needles in the dark, airless, smelly room as Corrie spoke to the eager group around her.

'With Jesus as your friend and Saviour, even this place can be filled with light. There is darkness in all our lives – not just in the lives of the guards. However good we are, each of us needs Jesus, the light of the world.'

They had been knitting several weeks now, and had found plenty of time for making friends and praying, talking and reading the Bible with the other women. The atmosphere in the dormitory was gradually changing.

The sisters were lying on their bunks, talking quietly before going to sleep.

'It was a good time of prayer tonight,' said Betsie.

'Yes, it was,' said Corrie. In the darkness her sister started to laugh softly.

'What's so funny?' Corrie asked.

'Well – you know you mentioned how surprised you were that guards hardly ever supervise us here.'

'Yes.'

'Well, I've found out why that is.'

'Go on.' Again, Betsie laughed.

'It's because of the fleas,' she chuckled. 'None of them like coming here because of the fleas.'

Corrie joined in with her sister's laughter.

'All right, you win,' she admitted, squeezing Betsie's hand. 'We do have to give thanks for everything. Goodnight.'

'Goodnight, Corrie.'

***

Betsie and Corrie were walking to roll call, hand-in-hand, praying as they went. They had found this walk with God helped them to bear the long, cold ordeal ahead. Above them shone the early morning stars. Around them lay the buildings of Ravensbruck – the barracks, the crematorium, the gas chambers, the guardhouse, the watchtowers, the bunkers, the hospital ... Yet in their hearts was such unbelievable peace that Betsie whispered, 'This is a bit of heaven, Corrie.'

They arrived at the place and were told to form ranks. Then began the endless calling out of names and numbers.

'What a sight we must look,' thought Corrie. 'Thousands of dishevelled, ragged-looking women.' Her own appearance was fairly typical. Her coat bulged oddly, where she had padded herself with newspaper to keep out the cold, and the hem was hanging down for the same reason. A dirty, checked cloth cap sat on her dull hair. Her legs were swollen through kidney disease brought on by poor prison food and made worse through hours of standing, and round them she had tied odd bits of knitting, while her shoes were almost worn through.

'At least the guards let us stamp our feet to keep from freezing up altogether,' she thought. But that wasn't much comfort today – since her feet were in a puddle. If she moved, a guard might rush at her, brandishing a whip. Besides, if she weren't there, someone else would be standing in the wet. Oh, how easy it would be to grow selfish in Ravensbruck. She remembered the well-meaning Dutch woman who had said to her as a new arrival, 'Look after yourself – that's the way to survive here.' But Corrie knew that was wrong. Jesus' way was to look after others.

Lorries rumbled into the space in front of them and suddenly the thousands of stamping feet were still. In terrible silence, the prisoners watched patients being helped out of the hospital barracks into the lorries, knowing that these sick people were about to go on a one-way journey.

Corrie stood there, feeling stunned and sickened. Seeing it with her own eyes brought home the full horror of it. These patients, some of whom were now being made comfortable by the more humane orderlies, were to be driven to the gas chambers and murdered. When the camp got too full, the sick were always the first to go, and after that it would be the turn of the people with red cards – like herself and Betsie and many of the other knitters.

'I can't bear all this suffering, Lord,' Corrie prayed. 'Teach me to take it to you and leave it with you – or I shall have no strength left to do your work here.'

Days, weeks, months passed with the weather getting colder all the time. In November, the prisoners were allowed a coat each. There was no news from loved ones, and only rumours passed from prisoner to prisoner, about the progress of the war. If they had known what was happening, it would have discouraged them even more, for that winter Hitler counter-attacked, slowing down the British and American troops. At the same time, he demanded more workers, more food and more goods for Germany, and his mad rage against the Jews reached its terrifying peak.

Corrie and Betsie could only guess at what was happening and go on with the work they believed God was calling them to do.

'When this is over,' said Betsie, 'we will have a big house in Holland and another in Germany, where people who have been broken by war will find healing.' She went on to describe the house she was picturing – its gardens, spacious rooms and beautiful woodwork.

'It's just as though she can see it,' Corrie thought. They were lying in bed after a busy, but happy Sunday. For once there had been no potato-planting or sand-shovelling to do, and they had had a few hours' free time between roll calls, which they had spent in Barracks 28, going from bunk to bunk, holding little services. There had been nine of them, one after the other, that day.

'It will be such a happy place,' Betsie finished.

'Yes,' agreed Corrie. 'We will have sports, music and activities, so that children can grow young again.'

'We will surround them with flowers and beautiful things.' said Betsie. 'We will need patience, but if they have been taught to hate, then, in time, they can be taught to love.'

'Taught to hate?' thought Corrie. Then the truth hit her. She had been talking about caring for their fellow-prisoners after the war, while Betsie had been thinking of the vicious brutal guards.

The prisoners for Barracks 28 were waiting to go indoors after a long, early morning roll call. For some reason, no one seemed to want to unlock the barracks door and let them in, so they were kept standing outside in the bitter cold for what seemed a long time.

A woman broke away from the group and tried to climb through a window. One of the guards dragged her away and beat her cruelly. Corrie shuddered and looked at Betsie. On some days she seemed to be shielded, somehow, from the full horror of her surroundings – but not today. Her face was full of suffering.

Corrie put her arms around her.

A mentally challenged child accidentally soiled her clothes, and was savagely beaten for it. Corrie felt as though the child's screams were tearing her apart, and, inside her arms, Betsie was wincing and shuddering. An old woman started pleading with the guard to be allowed in, but she was refused, curtly. A moment later, she crumpled on to the cold ground.

'Oh, Corrie,' Betsie whispered brokenly, 'this is hell.' Corrie wrapped her arms more tightly round her sister, and whispered back, 'God has promised to never, ever leave us.'

Then she looked up and saw that the dark clouds overhead were now reddening in the rays of the sun, soon to rise above the horizon and scatter the darkness.

After nearly an hour, the door was unlocked and the prisoners were allowed inside, to rest and thaw out. Betsie was soon her calm, serene self again, ready to listen to others and to tell them that Jesus was victorious, even here.

More and more prisoners were marching into Ravensbruck, evacuated from concentration camps in Austria, Belgium, France and Holland. The barracks were frighteningly, dangerously overcrowded.

In December, the days grew shorter and colder still, and the prisoners received another blanket each, but this didn't seem to make any difference to Betsie. She grew colder, paler and thinner every day, and her cough was dreadful to hear.

'I shall have to get her into hospital,' thought Corrie anxiously. 'Not that she'll receive any treatment there, or even any kindness, but at least she won't have the roll calls.'

She bent over her sister's bunk, rubbing her hands and stroking her forehead. Betsie had had a spell in hospital before, but this time she was far sicker – Corrie could see that. Her skin was looking almost transparent, and her heart beat sounded alarmingly faint and irregular.

'Roll call. Fall out all prisoners.' came the harsh shouting of the officials. Corrie and Maryke, a friend, cradled Betsie in their arms and carried her out.

'Wait.' called a guard. They stood still while she came across and stared down at Betsie's waxen face. Her own hard face seemed to soften just for a second, as she said, 'Take her back. I will order a stretcher and have her taken to hospital. Now go to roll call.'

Corrie was in agony to know what was happening to her sister. After roll call, she ran back to the dormitory. Betsie had been put on a stretcher and was being carried along the aisles. No one stopped Corrie as she walked along beside her.

They went out into the cold wintry air and across to the medical barracks. They walked past the long lines of sick, dead and dying, waiting outside the hospital, and then into a long ward.

The stretcher was put down on the floor. Betsie was speaking. Corrie bent down to hear her.

'We shall go everywhere telling people that there is no place on earth so dark that God's love cannot shine into it. They will believe us, because we have been here in Ravensbruck.' The voice was faint, but full of hope and certainty.

'When, Betsie, when?' asked Corrie.

'Soon, Corrie. By the new year we shall be free.'

It was these words, spoken a week before Christmas, which gave Corrie the courage to walk away from the hospital, back to the dormitory and the dreary knitting.

At midday, she had permission from 'The Snake' to visit, but a cruel nurse refused to allow her into the ward. She stood in the sleet looking in through the window at Betsie lying in a narrow cot nearby. Her lips were blue, but she was smiling brightly.

The afternoon and evening dragged by, with no chance of seeing her again. Corrie asked for permission, but was refused each time. Night fell, and Corrie slept badly.

Breakfast and roll call over, she went to the hospital. The suspense of not knowing was now unbearable.

She looked through the window near Betsie's bed, and saw two nurses lifting a body on a sheet – a body that was nothing but skin and bone.

Betsie's body.

PATIENT IN BARRACKS 9

Betsie was dead. Corrie stumbled away from the hospital barracks. After more than fifty years together, they were apart. Yet Betsie had said so firmly, 'By the new year, we shall be free, both of us, Corrie.'

'Well, Betsie is free now, but I am not. Here in this hell on earth I am utterly alone,' she thought, as she trudged blindly along on her swollen legs.

Winter in Ravensbruck without Betsie. How could she bear it?

Suddenly a memory stirred inside her head. Weeks before, Betsie had had to stay in hospital for a few days and she had left her there, her heart filled with angry questions. Why must they be in this evil place? Why must Betsie suffer so? And then she'd heard it – a voice speaking three words: 'Filled with tenderness'. She'd glanced around quickly, but there'd been no sign of the speaker, and in a great rush of joy she'd realised that the Lord himself had said the words, reassuring her that his heart held nothing but compassion for them both.

'The Lord has not changed,' she thought. 'He is still here. He still cares.'

Now she could go back and face the sight of Betsie's dead body. She returned to the medical barracks and got as far as the door of the washroom. Eleven corpses lay on the floor. It was too much. Once more she fled into the cold and walked aimlessly about.

Dimly she was aware of someone calling her name. And then her arm was being grasped and a voice was saying, 'Corrie, I've been looking everywhere for you. Come.' It was Mien. She led her to the hospital. She wanted to pull back, but Mien drew her over towards one of the bodies and urged, 'Look at her.'

Corrie forced her eyes downwards.

It was impossible ... unbelievable ... wonderful.

Betsie's face was a delight. Gone were the hollows and shadows of sickness and pain. Here was the Betsie of Haarlem – calm and beautiful.

'Oh, thank you, thank you, Lord, for this touch of your loving hand.' whispered Corrie. One last long look and she and Mien went out.

'We must tell the others,' Corrie said. 'Invite them to a memorial service.'

Corrie looked into the faces of the many women who loved Betsie and had gathered to remember her. For a few moments she struggled with her own emotions. Then she began to speak.

'Jesus, our Lord, went through death into a wonderful new life. Betsie has done the same. She is now with her Saviour, in the presence of her loved ones, free from all pain, and sickness and evil.'

She lay on her bunk, an aching space inside and beside her – Betsie's space. Pictures filled her mind one after another.

Betsie praying for the Germans while the bombs fell. Betsie producing a home-like atmosphere even in Barracks 28. Betsie praying, 'Lord remove this spirit of anger and fighting', while two women struggled and screamed – and then, amazingly, calmed down and sorted out their differences. Betsie – in hospital after a sleepless night through being constantly kicked out of bed by a French girl – saying earnestly, 'Corrie, there is such darkness in that poor child's life. I have been telling her that Jesus is victor and can help her'. Betsie looking round with a smile at the seething masses in Ravensbruck and saying, 'I am beginning to love the crowds'. Betsie shovelling sand, taunted and mimicked by the guards for not being able to carry as much as the others, answering sweetly, 'Let me do the little I can. If you make me carry more, I shan't be able to do anything at all'. Betsie looking at their brutal, sadistic warders, and saying, 'They have been taught to hate, so in time, they could be taught to love.' Betsie, eyes huge and bright in her deathly white face, whispering, 'We shall go everywhere telling people that there is no place on earth so dark that God's love cannot shine into it. They will believe us, because we have been here in Ravensbruck.' Betsie ... Betsie ... Betsie.

Corrie became aware of a voice around her.

'No, no, go away. We are full up.'

'There's no space here.'

She looked round and saw that the words were being addressed to a Russian woman who was looking for somewhere to sleep. Her face was sad and careworn. Corrie beckoned to her and the woman climbed into

Betsie's space with a smile of thanks. Corrie knew very little Russian, but two words she did know.

'Jesoes Christoes?' she said softly. The Russian woman's face lit up and she threw her arms round her new friend.

***

'Get up. Time for roll call.'

It was not yet half-past four on Sunday morning, the day after Betsie's death. Corrie struggled out of bed and went out into the cold. Her heart lifted at the sight of the glowing sky as the sun rose above the horizon. She got into line with others and the numbering began.

'Someone is missing.' shouted the guard, and the whole process began all over again. The hours dragged by. Corrie and several other women began to feel ill.

'Thank you, Father, that Betsie isn't having to stand here in this freezing cold,' she prayed ...

They had been standing at attention for six and a half hours when they heard, at last, the word: 'Dismissed'. Corrie staggered into the barracks and collapsed on to the bunk.

'Did they find the missing prisoner?' she asked the people near her. One of them answered grimly, 'Oh, yes, they found her all right. And the reason she wasn't at roll call was that she was lying dead in her bunk – and we get punished for that.'

'Number 66730 prisoner ten Boom Cornelia, come forward.'

'What now?' Corrie wondered.

'Stand on one side.' she was told. She obeyed and the roll call began. It was three days since Betsie's death. Corrie wondered why she was being singled out.

She glanced at the young girl standing next to her and whispered, 'What do you think will happen to me?'

'Death sentence,' the girl whispered back.

Corrie was not afraid to die. Meeting Betsie and her father and mother and the Lord they loved would be heaven. But perhaps this would be her last chance to speak to the girl beside her.

'I'm Corrie,' she whispered. 'What's your name?'

'Tiny.'

'God loves you, Tiny,' Corrie told her very softly. 'He sent his Son Jesus to die for you, so that you can go to be with him in heaven after you die. All you need to do is to invite Jesus into your life to take away your sins and be your Saviour and Guide. Will you do that, Tiny?'

'I will.'

Roll call lasted three hours and all that time Corrie and Tiny talked ...

'Get into your workgroups.' shouted the guard. Roll call was over. To Corrie he said, 'Follow me.' He led her into the office barracks. The man at the desk looked up as Corrie stepped in front of him.

'Discharged,' he said, stamping a card.

Discharged. Free. She couldn't take it in.

'You will report for medical inspection first,' said the guard, and he led the little group of prisoners down the corridor. Corrie took off her clothes and stood naked as usual before the doctor. He looked coldly down her thin, shivering body, and then at her legs, badly swollen, thanks to the last long roll call.

'Oedema,' he barked. 'Barracks 9.'

It was a cruel blow. Just when she was beginning to grasp that she really would be set free at last – her hopes had been smashed. Now it might be weeks or months before she was released – if ever. The Nazis would only send prisoners out if they looked fit and well.

She was taken to Barracks 9, one of the hospital barracks, and left in a ward. She walked slowly down it, looking at the faces of those around her, but already what she was hearing told her the kind of place this was. On either side lay women in terrible pain. Some were the badly injured survivors of a prison train bombed on its way to Ravensbruck. In the middle of the ward on a table, one woman was being worked on by doctors and nurses. She was fully conscious and screaming, yet their faces held no trace of concern. Some able-bodied German women, and others who might have gone to help the patients who were moaning or crying out in pain, seemed utterly indifferent, or worse. A sick woman let out a long wail of anguish and a German girl mimicked her. Her friends burst out into coarse, cackling laughter.

On a top bunk, two Hungarians were talking noisily. Their faces were dark and evil. Suddenly one of them thrust out a gangrenous foot, as though to infect the new arrival.

Corrie reached a free bunk and collapsed on it in utter shock and horror.

'Lord,' she prayed, 'protect me, help me. I thought I had seen everything, but this so-called hospital is a torture-chamber. The pain and evil here is too much for me. When will it end?'

Sleep that night was impossible. All around her, women moaned or screamed in agony. Others kept repeating a German word. Corrie couldn't understand it, but clearly the women were pleading for something. Wouldn't anyone get it for them?

Many times she heard patients staggering weakly to the toilet next door and then back again. And three times she heard a sickening thud.

In the morning, she learnt that these were the sounds of women falling from the top bunks to their deaths on the hard, cold floor – women who had been trying to reach the toilets.

'My father's case again.' she thought, and prayed, 'Lord, I cannot bear this. Bear it for me please.'

She went across and spoke to a French girl.

'What was it the women kept calling for in the night?' she asked.

'Bedpans,' the girl replied. Corrie thought, 'At least that is one job I can take on.'

She went over to the bunk opposite hers where there was a mentally handicapped child. Her body was wasted and skeleton-like, but her face was lovely and framed by soft curls.

Corrie took her hands and said, 'My name is Corrie. Tell me yours.'

'Oelie,' the child replied.

'Are you sick, Oelie?' Corrie asked, gently.

The girl turned round and pulled up her dress to show her back. Corrie was almost overcome with horror at the wound barely covered by toilet paper.

'What kind of terrible operation has this poor child been through?' she wondered, repressing a shudder. She pulled the dress down and smiled into the wide eyes.

'How old are you, Oelie?'

'Fifteen.'

'Young in years, but old in suffering,' thought Corrie.

'Jesus loved you so much that he died for you and came alive again and now he's busy getting ready a little house for you in heaven,' she told the girl. 'Oh, you will love heaven, Oelie. There are no bad people there and you won't have any more pain ...'

Just like the rest of her 'special' children, Oelie was drinking in every word.

'Now I know why you have sent me to Barracks 9, Lord,' Corrie said in her prayer-time that night.

Someone called for a bedpan and she got up, found one, and took it to her. The patient looked into her face as though she couldn't believe what she was seeing.

'Oh, you are good.' she whispered. 'I didn't know there could be anyone good in this place.' Corrie waited and then removed the bedpan and emptied it.

She passed near one of the prisoners who'd been on the bombed prison train, and stopped in sudden shock. The poor woman only had one leg and part of her back had been blown off, too. Gently, Corrie lifted her thin, mutilated body and made her more comfortable.

The days dragged by. One of them was December 25th – Christmas. Corrie spent her time helping the other patients, and telling them about Jesus. Every evening she told Oelie more about her home in heaven. And each night she looked after the bedpans.

One night these articles were missing. 'Is this the German girls' idea of a joke?' Corrie wondered. She pleaded with them, and with the Hungarian women, to hand over the pans, but they only laughed at her.

Corrie lay awake, feeling helpless as patients kept calling out. Then the French girl spoke up: 'They've hidden them under their blankets'. Corrie knew that the 'they' referred to the two Hungarian women whose bunks were above her. She got out of bed to speak to them, when a terrified scream came from the French girl. The sobbing girl pointed to the Hungarian woman with the gangrenous foot and said, 'She flung her bandage in my face.'

Corrie looked up and heard a coarse laugh as something hit her cheek.

'Ugh. The puss-filled bandage,' she thought, revolted, and hurried to wash her face again and again.

'How can I go back for the bedpans, now?' she wondered. But she did. As the Hungarians saw her coming towards them, they flung the bedpans on to the floor. Corrie picked them up and went on with her job.

Seven of the longest days and nights in Corrie's life passed. The only thing she was spared, as a patient, were the roll calls. Instead, there were the naked medical inspections.

She stood in front of the doctor once more. Her heart beat quickly as he looked at her legs.

'Discharged,' he said. Was she really being set free this time? Corrie felt dazed as she stepped out of Barracks 9, on to the snowy ground. There the horrible reality of Ravensbruck hit her again.

On the cold, white ground lay the body of a young and lovely girl – a sick prisoner who, like so many others, had died before she'd managed to reach the hospital. Corrie's heart ached for all that she must have suffered.

She followed the guard into a room where there were piles of clean clothes. Friendly prisoners helped her into fresh underwear, a skirt, blouse, shoes, hat and overcoat.

A package was handed to her. In it were her clothes and some of Betsie's, from Scheveningen. Then there was a form to sign, saying she had never had an accident, never been sick or badly treated.

'There will be an end to these lies – to all this evil,' Corrie comforted herself as she signed.

The little party of eight German and two Dutch women were taken to the gates. Corrie was amazed that the other Hollander had been released, for she looked so ill. Her name was Clare.

There was a wait before the heavy doors were opened. As Corrie stood there, Mimi passed and whispered, 'Tiny is dead.'

'Keep away.' the guard shouted at her, and he ordered Corrie to face the gate. She obeyed, but his harsh voice could not spoil her happiness at knowing that Tiny had died trusting Jesus.

The gates swung open and out they marched. In an outer office, they paused to collect their belongings. Corrie was handed her money, her ring and watch.

Then they were on their way to the station. The snow crunched under their feet and all around them lay a winter wonderland. Childhood memories of skating and snow games flashed through Corrie's mind.

She was quickly out of breath as they climbed out of the valley and Clare looked ready to drop.

'Look at the two Dutch women hobbling along.' jeered the young German girls. 'We Germans have got twice as much grit as you.'

'We're not free yet,' Corrie thought. 'The evil of Ravensbruck is still close to us, even in this beautiful countryside.'

There was a wonderful view of snow-covered lakes and trees. The pines to the left could have been a picture on a Christmas card, but under their branches were rows and rows of women in prison clothes, being driven along by overseers.

'Girls from the guard house,' thought Corrie, with sympathy. To them fell the heavy work of wood chopping, coal carrying and road making.

They arrived at the station and the guard left them. They were on their own. Corrie felt helpless and confused. How could she possibly get herself and her sick companion through Germany and back to Holland?

Somehow, on New Year's Day, they found themselves in Berlin. The scars of war lay right across the once-beautiful city. After that, there were hours of waiting for trains, finding the right platforms, and travelling on and on. Germany had become a wasteland. Corrie saw it all through a haze of weariness, weakness and hunger. Her bread ration had either been stolen, or accidentally dropped. She was forced to beg for food, but found people hard-hearted and suspicious.

At last, in a small-town station, a Red Cross nurse, risking punishment, gave her a bowl of thick soup intended for a soldier. Later, at a large station, she met a kind-hearted officer who arranged for her and Clare to have a meal in a friendly home.

Corrie thanked God for these exceptions to the general callousness.

'The damage that has been done here to people is far worse than the damage to cities,' she thought.

'Oh Clare, we are crossing the border. We are in Holland at last.' Corrie exclaimed. Her pale companion smiled back at her, and Corrie went on, 'Here in our own dear country, things will be different. I'm sure of it.'

⏱ THE HOMECOMING ⏱

The train stopped at Groningen, a small Dutch town, and the two weak, dishevelled women struggled out , and made their way to a Christian hospital near the station.

Corrie rang the bell. The door was opened and a nurse stood there. One look at her face, and Corrie knew that all was well. Here was someone dedicated to caring.

'Come in.' she said, kindly.

Corrie was soaking in a warm bath. There was a knock at the door and a voice called, 'Are you ready?'

She answered, 'Just a few minutes more, Truus, it's such bliss.' and heard a laughing, 'All right', in reply.

She couldn't stop staring round the bathroom. How pretty and clean and fresh it smelt. Oh, it was wonderful to be in Holland among kind people again. She knew that at this moment Clare was lying between crisp, clean sheets, receiving the care she needed.

She looked at her skin. There were still flea-bites, but the dirt and grime had gone.

'Clean skin and a full stomach – what blessings.' she thought.

She lay back again and relived the meal she had just eaten. Potatoes, sprouts, meat, gravy, all piping hot, and followed by a pudding and an apple. Once, in Ravensbruck, she had said to Betsie, 'We'll have to be very careful about what we eat at first, when we get out of here.' But Betsie had answered, 'No, Corrie, we will be able to eat what we like. God will take care of that.' How right she had been.

'Fancy one of the nurses being a youth leader I knew. Dear Truus Benes. I'm not surprised she didn't recognise me at first,' thought Corrie, with a smile, picturing her lank hair and dirty appearance.

With a sigh, she stepped out of the bath, wrapped herself in a soft, clean towel, and called, 'I'm ready.'

Truus, and some of the other nurses, helped her to dress in the clothes they had found. Gently, lovingly, they kitted her out. There were even pins for her hair. She accepted their help gladly, and even laughed out loud for sheer joy.

Truus led her into a room with bright curtains and colour-washed walls. Against one of them was a bed, a real bed, with clean sheets, fluffy blankets and soft pillows. Nearby was a shelf with a row of books.

Corrie stood still, trying to take everything in. So many blessings all at once almost overwhelmed her.

Truus led her gently to the bed, saying, 'Rest – that's what you need now, I am sure.' She helped Corrie take off her shoes and lie down. Then she tucked a soft pillow under her swollen feet and covered her with a light blanket.

'If you need anything, just let me know,' she said.

Left alone in the room, Corrie lay still and let the tears of joy come ...

She was too excited to sleep. There were so many beautiful things to see. And she could hear delightful sounds – children laughing, a distant chiming of bells, a woman singing, the music of Bach from a nearby radio ... Now at last she could believe she was really free.

But the war was not over. Back in Ravensbruck, a week after Corrie's release, all women of her age were put to death, and it was discovered that Prisoner 66730 had been set free through a mistake in the records – a clerical error.

Knowing nothing of this yet, Corrie stayed for ten days in the hospital, dreaming of seeing her family again.

'We are doing our best to arrange transport for you to Hilversum,' the hospital superintendent told her, 'but it's not easy. As you know, very few people are allowed private cars these days.'

'I quite understand,' said Corrie. 'And I'm so grateful to you for everything.' She had managed to get a message to Willem telling him of her release and Betsie's death – but she longed to be with him and all her loved ones.

'Corrie – we have arranged it.' said Truus, one day. 'You will travel on a food truck this evening. No headlights, of course, it's an illegal journey.'

It was an exciting ride through the dark, and then came the reunion in Willem and Tine's nursing home. The hugging and kissing went on for a long time.

'So many joys, I can hardly bear it,' thought Corrie, surrounded by her nephews and nieces, with Willem and Tine close by.

After the first few moments, she noticed, with a sudden sense of shock, how ill Willem looked. She took his hands and looked lovingly at him – wanting to know but not daring to ask about the missing member of the family.

'No, Corrie, we've had no news of Kik,' said Willem, answering her unspoken question. A shadow fell across the room.

'You can stay here as long as you like, Corrie,' said Willem, 'but I know you will want to get back to a certain little house in Haarlem.'

'And a certain big sister and her husband and family,' added Corrie.

'Well, I've arranged the journey,' said her brother. 'I'm still allowed a car within limits, so I can drive you part of the way, and then Pickwick will take over.'

Pickwick was an old friend of the family, and also an underground leader. Corrie was thrilled to see him again and talk over old times as they drove along.

They were in Haarlem at last. Corrie leaned out of the window, eager for her first sight of the river and the bridges, the market-square and St Bavo's, the familiar streets and shops.

'Oh Pickwick, there's my own little home.' she exclaimed, seeing the corner house and watch shop again. 'Thank you so much.'

She climbed out of the car and sped up to the front door. Could it really be not quite a year since she had left this place? In some ways it seemed a lifetime ago ...

Nollie and her girls were waiting to welcome her, and there was another long, happy reunion.

'We've cleaned the house from top to bottom,' her nieces told her proudly.

'You dear girls – thank you.' said Corrie.

'There were homeless families living here for a time but it's all yours again now,' said Nollie. 'Come and look round – I know you're dying to.'

She was right. Corrie wanted to see and touch everything. Memories flooded back as she walked into each room. The sight of Father's chair brought a stab of pain. She ran her fingers lovingly over it, then moved on to the piano, the pictures, the cupboards ...

'I'm afraid the cat disappeared and never came back,' Nollie said. 'And the Nazis stole your typewriter and some rugs and books.'

They went into the workshop. Nollie said, 'We have managed to keep the business going – but your workbench is empty and all ready for you.' Corrie went across to it, with tears in her eyes.

Corrie was watchmaking again, and in charge of some very efficient repair men, trained under her father.

What happy months these had been for her. True, the war was not over, the weather was bitterly cold, and food and most other things were very scarce, but she was home, surrounded by friends and loved ones, and picking up the threads of her life – working in the house and shop, teaching children and young people's groups, speaking at meetings ...

And she had not forgotten crazy Thys, Hank, Oelie or any of the others. Her home was now a refuge for children like them who had been hiding for years in attics or even cupboards. They still could not walk about openly, but Corrie was able to give them loving care.

She followed the progress of the war as closely as she could. Bleak February seemed brighter for knowing that British and American troops had recovered from Hitler's counter-attacks, and were pressing northward from the Alps, while the Red Army was entering Germany from Poland.

In March, she learned the exciting news that American troops had reached the Rhine and were capturing one German city after another. In April, it was known that the Russians were in Berlin, only a few streets away from the bunker where Hitler was hiding. It was clear that he had lost everything except a few loyal people and his undying rage and hatred. Then came the news that he had shot himself. She was relieved, but not surprised to hear, a week later, that his successor had surrendered.

World War Two was over. The streets of Haarlem were thronged with people, waving flags and singing the national anthem. Corrie stood in the market-square among them, as happy as anyone there.

Something was happening in front of the town hall, she noticed. A girl was being dragged up the steps by several people. The next moment one of them was cutting her hair, while the crowd jeered. Now someone else had come forward with a tin of orange paint. He was pouring it all over her ...

Corrie turned away, saddened, and began threading her way through the crowd.

'Obviously the girl must have co-operated with the Germans, and been a traitor to her own country,' she thought, 'but repaying evil for evil is not Jesus' way.'

Slowly, she walked through the streets, thinking, 'The war is over, but the darkness which caused it is still present. The damage it has done can be seen everywhere.' She thought of bombed cities and scarred countryside, of the millions who had been killed in the fighting, and in the camps. She thought of the suffering survivors – those who had lost homes and loved ones, or become crippled in mind, body or spirit …

It was good to reach her home and go inside to think and pray.

***

Corrie was cycling home after speaking at a meeting on the outskirts of Haarlem. More and more now, she was going round telling people what she and Betsie had learnt in prison and concentration camp. Today, as usual, everyone had listened eagerly.

It was spring. The landscape was not as beautiful as it would have been at this time of the year before the war.

Many trees had been cut down for fuel, and fields which should have been blazing with colour were bare, for the Dutch people had had to eat their own flower bulbs. Even so, there were still stretches of unspoilt loveliness.

Corrie paused to admire a few poplars and a windmill against the light sky. At their feet lay a wide meadow fringed by a pool where dabchicks and waterfowl skimmed and dived.

'Once upon a time before the war,' she thought, 'that meadow would have held some handsome cows.'

She started pedalling again. She would be home soon. Somehow, she didn't feel overjoyed at the thought.

'What's the matter with me?' she wondered. 'I love my home dearly, so why, nowadays, do I feel restless when I'm there?' She missed the children, of course, but it wasn't just that.

Holland, like the other war-damaged countries, had started on the long task of getting things back to normal – clearing rubble, rebuilding schools, factories, shops, offices ... So when schools for the handicapped had restarted, Corrie's children had gone back to them to live and be taught and cared for, openly and fully.

She was glad, for their sakes, although she missed their love and trust, and she still had family, friends and work.

And yet ... had she been through Scheveningen, Vught and Ravensbruck, only to settle back into her old way of life?

Surely not.

⏱ MISSIONARY TO ALL ⏱
THE WORLD

Corrie was free. Free to work and visit friends. Free to stand and stare at storks on the river Spaarne, or walk along the sand dunes listening to the majestic music of the sea, free to worship in dear old St Bavo's cathedral, free to travel and speak at meetings, openly.

But she was not free from memories. Often, as she lay awake in her own clean, comfortable bed, pictures would start flashing across the screen of her mind. Some brought deep sadness and tears ...

Father dying in a prison corridor. The girls behind the guardhouse walls where the regular thuds and screams of a flogging could so often be heard. The women sentenced to be used in horrifying medical experiments – sitting in the barracks, waiting. Herself and Betsie naked at medical inspections. A half-dead zombie, just released from the punishment bunker where he'd been kept for days without food, water, light, or room to move. People lying dead on the ground outside the hospital barracks. A child, a sick person, an old person being ill-treated. The beatings, the shootings, the death trucks.

But there were other memories ... Lieutenant Rahms and a few officers and guards like himself who cared and stayed human. Mien, Maryke, Mimi and dozens of others who went on loving and helping and hoping. Tiny, Marie, Willy, Diet, and so many more whose lives were changed as they turned to Jesus and let his love fill them – so that Barracks 28 became known as 'that crazy place where people hope'. The times of prayer and Bible reading, singing and worship, when God was so real and close that they were filled with peace and even joy. The miracles which gave added proof that he cared – the Bible and underwear the guards didn't see ... the vitamin drops ... Betsie. Her life had been a daily miracle, and then there had been that last sight of her face – beautiful again in death. That was a memory to treasure with so many others.

Suddenly Corrie knew why she had been feeling so restless. Of course. God was calling her to do the work she and Betsie had talked and prayed and dreamt about in Ravensbruck – the work of providing beautiful, caring homes for people damaged by war, and spreading the message that God had given them everywhere.

***

Corrie was standing outside a magnificent house set in beautiful grounds in Bloemendaal. It was a glorious June day and her heart was full of joy. Betsie's vision had turned into reality. The fifty-six roomed mansion behind her had been offered by a woman who had heard her speak. God had sent money to buy it and helpers to run it, and now it was filling up with concentration camp survivors and others crippled in some way by the war.

She found it thrilling to see some of them already beginning to heal inside and out, as they opened their hearts to God's love and started to live normal lives.

She could see one of the residents working on a flower bed. Betsie had always believed that growing flowers could be a way back to normality. 'How right she was.' thought Corrie. And this lovely house, with its beautiful woodwork – how accurately Betsie had described it.

'If only Betsie was with me. She was so sure that we would be working together after the war,' she thought.

Suddenly it struck her that they were working together – in a way. Betsie's words and influence were inspiring her all the time.

A nurse came out and said, 'Oh, there you are, Corrie. I wanted a word with you.'

'Hullo, Ellen,' answered Corrie, with a smile. 'Is anything wrong?'

'Well, it's one of the patients. He's wandering about at all hours of the night. Do you think ...'

'No, Ellen,' Corrie interrupted gently, but firmly. 'No rules, no restrictions. These people must be given time and space to work out their inner hurts in their own way. Please bear with them, however unconventional they are.'

'I understand,' said the nurse, slowly, and walked back inside. Corrie followed her saying, 'I couldn't resist a few moments in the sunshine, but I'd better get back to work now. Have you heard what we're planning to do next?'

The nurse shook her head, and the two of them moved up the wide staircase as Corrie said, 'The idea is that I shall open up my home to ex-Dutch Nazis.'

The girl gave a little gasp, and Corrie went on, 'Yes, I know it won't be popular, but I'm sure it's right. People who have betrayed their countrymen are just as much in need of love as our friends here are. Besides, the folk in Bloemendaal need to learn to forgive not only the Germans but their fellow-Dutchmen for the wrongs they have done.'

'It won't be easy for them,' Ellen commented.

'No, it won't,' agreed Corrie. 'But Betsie and I saw so clearly in camp that forgiving our enemies is the way back to peace and joy, and that God gives us the strength to do this when we open our lives to him and his love.'

'Well, I hope it all goes well,' said Ellen. 'Are you off on your travels soon?'

'Yes,' said Corrie. 'And I'm quite nervous. To start globe-trotting at my age seems rather strange, but what God taught us in Ravensbruck needs to be heard all round the world – if God gives me strength.'

***

Corrie was unpacking her case in a hotel room in America. For almost ten months she had been travelling around the country, speaking to large and small groups about what God had taught her, and the work he was helping her to do in Holland.

People had been eager to listen and to help, by prayer and gifts.

'The Lord has led me step by step, and it's been a wonderful time,' thought Corrie, 'but I'm homesick for Holland. And perhaps, after being at home for a while, I could travel around the other countries of Europe – anywhere except Germany.'

She undressed and got into bed.

As she lay there on the edge of sleep, she remembered something Betsie had said.

'Corrie, we must take the love of Jesus to the Germans after the war,' she had whispered. 'There are many concentration camps in Germany. I have asked the Lord to give us one of these to make into a home where the Germans can be taught to love again.'

Corrie's eyes stung with tears, as she seemed to see again Betsie's frail form under the threadbare prison blanket, and hear her hopeful, eager voice.

'All right, Lord. If you want me to go to Germany, I will do it, in your strength,' she prayed.

***

Corrie was in a concentration camp again – Darmstadt, not Ravensbruck. But now there were no concrete walls or barbed wire coils, and the compounds were filled flower beds. The barracks were still standing, no longer grime-grey, but bright with fresh paint and flower-decked window boxes. Another of Betsie's visions had become reality. Darmstadt, in Germany, was now a home for needy, homeless, helpless people.

Corrie spent many hours there, and today she was going from room to room, trying to get to know the sad occupants. In one cubicle was a German who had been a lawyer before the war. Now he sat in a wheelchair all day, staring dully into space. Corrie sat down opposite him, and saw at once what was blocking his recovery.

'There is only one way to deal with bitterness – give it up.' she said simply.

He turned to look coldly at her.

'How would you know?' he asked, his voice hard.

'During the war, a Dutchman betrayed me, my family, and many of our friends,' she began. 'We were arrested and put in prison. Ten days later, my father died. My heart was filled with hatred for the man who had caused our suffering. But at last I handed over my hate and bitterness and God filled me with his love. I forgave that man. Through him my sister and I were sent to Ravensbruck. We suffered greatly and my sister died there. But I heard that Jan Vogel had been sentenced to death. I wrote and told him that I forgave him, and that God would forgive him and give him a new life and hope if he would turn to him. And he did.'

Corrie stopped speaking. The man was looking at her with a very changed expression.

'I must think about what you say,' he said, quietly.

***

Corrie went all round Germany speaking and counselling. She found the people utterly changed. The arrogant soldiers, with their hard hats and stony hearts, had gone. They were now in disgrace. Many were in prison. She heard that Lieutenant Rahms was now in an internment camp, and immediately sat down to write to those in charge, telling them how good he had been to their family, and asking for him to be set free.

'With permission I will take him and his family into our house in Holland,' she added.

Her request was not granted.

'Poor Hans Rahms,' she thought. 'He did his best to be just and kind, but now he is put with the people who committed atrocious crimes in the cause of Nazism.'

'Some must be suffering horribly as they see clearly for the first time the appalling things they have done, in their blind devotion to Hitler,' she realised.

The ordinary German people, who welcomed her into their homes and listened eagerly to her talks, were suffering too, she knew. When the truth about the concentration camps proved to be worse than even the wildest rumours, most were as horrified as the rest of the world. Ninety-six thousand women died in Ravensbruck alone, and that was only one camp. There were also Belsen, Buchenwold, Dachau, Belsec, Chelmno, Treblinka – and Auschwitz where, for the past four years, six thousand Jews a day had been taken into four gas chambers, and slowly, painfully murdered. In the course of the war, at least six million of Europe's Jews had been killed by the Nazis.

'No wonder so many Germans are shocked and despairing.' thought Corrie, as she walked, or was driven, through bomb-blackened cities.

Munich was one such city. Corrie spoke to a large crowd there – passing on the message of hope that God had given her for the German people, as well as for everyone else. 'Forgiveness is what we all need to receive and to give. Jesus can help us to forgive our enemies, and even to love them ...' she said.

Afterwards, she stood at the door of the hall to shake hands with the people at the meeting.

A man stepped up to her.

'Thank you for your message,' he said. 'I have asked Jesus into my life.'

Corrie stiffened. Suddenly she was back in Ravensbruck. She and Betsie were walking naked in front of a guard with hard eyes and a sneering mouth. It was this man. And now he was saying, 'I was a guard at Ravensbruck once and you said you had spent some time there. God has forgiven me for the terrible things I did in that place, but I need your forgiveness too, Miss ten Boom – please.'

He held out his hand. Corrie stood as though turned to stone. Shake this man by the hand after all the misery he had caused Betsie and thousands like her? Impossible. And yet she was always telling people to forgive their enemies. It had been her message in the meeting which had only just ended.

Without closing her eyes, she prayed silently, 'Lord, I can take his hand, but I can't change my feelings. Only you can do that.' Then she raised her arm and took his outstretched hand in her own. Their eyes met, and a sudden feeling of warmth flowed down her arm, and then through her whole body, melting her.

'I forgive you with all my heart,' she said to the man, and was amazed that she meant every word. With eyes full of tears, she watched him walk away – forgiven.

***

'Mr Rahms, how good to see you.' said Corrie. This was one German she had wanted to meet during her travels, and here they were at last, face to face.

He looked much older, but there was the same friendliness in his expression.

They talked together, and then Corrie asked, 'Tell me, did you receive Jesus as your Saviour?'

'No,' he answered, 'but I never forgot what you told me, or your sister's prayers.'

Eagerly, Corrie spoke to him again of the light of Jesus which she longed for him to have in his life. It was hard for him to see his need, because he had always done his best. But, in the end, he understood.

To Corrie's great joy, he prayed that Jesus would come into his life.

Corrie was back in Darmstadt. The German lawyer met her at the station, driving a car that had been specially adapted for him.

'How are you?' Corrie asked him.

'Fine,' he answered. 'And I want you to know that I gave my bitterness to God and he has filled me with his love. Now I work at the refugee camp, and am finding out that God can use even a legless man.'

'That's great news.' said Corrie, beaming.

A shadow crossed the man's face, as he asked, 'Does your bitterness ever come back, after you have given it to God?'

'Oh, yes,' said Corrie. 'Over and over again. But each time I hand it straight back to him and press on, depending on Jesus for victory, and he gives it to me.'

The lawyer's face brightened, as he answered, 'Oh, I am glad to hear you say that. When my hate and bitterness come back, I will do the same, now.'

**

Corrie woke up in a strange hotel bedroom. Just for a moment, she couldn't think where she was. Then she remembered the name of the town and the details of the meetings she would be taking.

'I wonder how much longer the Lord wants me to live this gypsy life?' she mused.

Was it really possible that more than thirty years had gone since the war? She thought about those years of travelling – sometimes alone, sometimes with a close friend ...

Twice round the world, visiting every continent and more than sixty countries.

'And I must have slept in a thousand different beds – not all as comfortable as this one,' she said to herself, remembering nights spent on a straw mat on a mud floor in India.

'So many different meetings.' she thought. Small groups, big groups – in homes, churches, halls, prisons, streets, theatres, universities, stadiums ... but the same message of love and forgiveness in each. And now there were books and films carrying that message to millions of people she would never have a chance to meet.

Just now, she was feeling a little homesick for Holland. She had been back many times over the years to see her family and friends and to visit Bloemendaal and another centre which had been bought for the work of rehabilitating people. When the homes were no longer needed for those who had suffered during the war, they had been opened to mentally handicapped children and others in need of special help.

Willem had died not long after the war and Nollie more recently, but she still felt close to the rest of her family – and to her homeland.

She was proud of the way Holland had kept what was best in its old way of life, while accepting new ideas, so that now it could compete with other countries in world-markets and even give a lead – in the way it planned out its growing cities, fought pollution and organised big companies. Every time Corrie returned, she saw fresh signs of progress.

On one visit she met and talked to Princess Wilhelmina, as she preferred to be called now that she had abdicated so that her daughter Juliana could become Queen.

'How proud Father would have been that his daughter should have the honour of staying with this great lady,' Corrie thought.

She couldn't get used to being so well-known round the world, through the books and films about her. In her own mind she was still very much the watchmaker's daughter from Haarlem. But the little house and watch shop were no longer her home. It was now a museum for people from all over the world to visit. Instead, she was a welcome guest in homes all over the world. But though she loved these places and had friends everywhere, she knew that her true home was somewhere else. More and more these days she thought of some favourite words of her father's:

'When Jesus takes your hand, he keeps you tight. When Jesus keeps you tight, he leads you through life. When Jesus leads you through life, he brings you safely home.'

It was that home she longed for now. But until the Lord took her there, she had work to do for him here on earth.

She got out of bed and started to dress, thinking and praying about what she would say to the people who would soon be gathering to hear her.

'Lord,' she prayed, 'fill me with your Holy Spirit, so that I can help them to see that Jesus is victor. Amen.'

Hall of Faith

Therefore, since we are surrounded by so great a cloud of witnesses ...

—Heb. 12:1

WE have been blessed to know and share the stories of many who have lived faithful lives in obedience to the will of God. While not everyone whose stories are told in the Hall of Faith series have entered their eternal rest, everyone has a story from which we can learn of the grace of God.

The Hall of Faith series seeks to edify the people of God through short, narrative-driven biographies of Christians, whether from ages past or the modern day.

Also available from Christian Focus
in the Hall of Faith series ...

Billy Graham

by Catherine Mackenzie

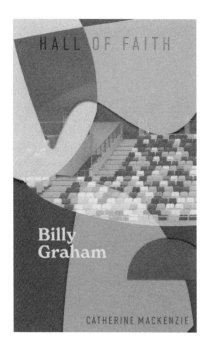

978-1-5271-1158-5

Witness Billy Graham's journey from humble beginnings
on a North Carolina farm to becoming one of the most
influential figures of the twentieth century.

Dietrich Bonhoeffer

by Dayspring MacLeod

978-1-5271-1052-6

The thrilling tale of the German preacher who plotted to assassinate Hitler.

Joni Eareckson Tada

by Catherine Mackenzie

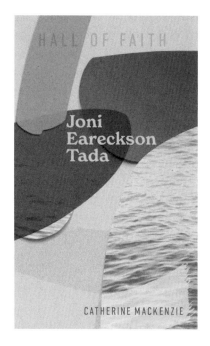

978-1-5271-1053-3

A deep dive into human suffering and God's goodness.

Christian Focus Publications

Our mission statement –

STAYING FAITHFUL

In dependence upon God we seek to impact the world through literature faithful to His infallible Word, the Bible. Our aim is to ensure that the Lord Jesus Christ is presented as the only hope to obtain forgiveness of sin, live a useful life and look forward to heaven with Him.

Our Books are published in four imprints:

CHRISTIAN FOCUS

popular works including biographies, commentaries, basic doctrine and Christian living.

CHRISTIAN HERITAGE

books representing some of the best material from the rich heritage of the church.

MENTOR

books written at a level suitable for Bible College and seminary students, pastors, and other serious readers. The imprint includes commentaries, doctrinal studies, examination of current issues and church history.

CF4•K

children's books for quality Bible teaching and for all age groups: Sunday school curriculum, puzzle and activity books; personal and family devotional titles, biographies and inspirational stories – Because you are never too young to know Jesus.

Christian Focus Publications Ltd,
Geanies House, Fearn, Ross-shire,
IV20 1TW, Scotland, United Kingdom.
www.christianfocus.com